Blanche of Castile

and the

Holy Blood Holy Grail

By Thomas P. Miller

*

*　　　　*

Blanche of Castile

and the

Holy Blood Holy Grail

By Thomas P. Miller

Blanche of Castile and the Holy Blood Holy Grail

Table of Contents

Introduction

Genealogies

Blanche of Castile and the Holy Blood Holy Grail

*

*   *

INTRODUCTION

In the two books, Holy Blood, Holy Grail, (1982), and
The Messianic Legacy, (1986), both books by Michael Baigent,
Richard Leigh, and Henry Lincoln, there is mention made of
Blanche of Castile, and a genealogy parchment dated 1244, bearing
the seal of Blanche of Castile. This parchment was said to be one of
four parchments discovered in 1891 by Berenger Sauniere, priest of
the parish church of Mary Magdalene, in the French village of
Rennes-Le-Chateau, near the southern border of France.

These four parchments were said to be discovered when Berenger
Sauniere was repairing and rebuilding and renovating the parish
church of Rennes-Le-Chateau. Two of the parchments were
described as genealogies, the first parchment dated 1244, bearing the
seal of Blanche of Castile, and the second parchment dated 1644, by
Francois-Pierre d'Hautpoul, Lord of Rennes-Le-Chateau.

The other two parchments were said to be written in the 1780's by
Abbe Antoine Bigou, priest of Rennes-Le-Chateau. At the time of
the writing of the two books, Holy Blood, Holy Grail, (1982), and
The Messianic Legacy, (1986), and in earlier books published in
French, and in many subsequent books published in English,
written about Berenger Sauniere and Rennes-Le-Chateau, and
written about the 1950's and the later organization known as the
Priory of Sion, it is stated and explained that the two parchments
said to be written in the 1780's by Abbe Antoine Bigou, priest of
Rennes-Le-Chateau, were Latin texts containing excerpts from the
New Testament, and that these two Latin texts contained encoded
secret messages, which were subsequently decoded.

These Latin texts were first published in a book in 1967 by Gerard
De Sede, an author associated with the Priory of Sion, and later
published by many other book authors.

However, it was later discovered that at least one of the Latin texts was from a version of the New Testament found in Codex Bezae, an old manuscript first published in 1895. And an associate of the Priory of Sion, a man named Philippe De Cherisey, (d.1985), in an interview after 1982 with writer Jean-Luc Chaumeil, claimed that he had fabricated the two Latin text parchments, apparently in 1956, using a version of Gospel texts in the Dictionary of Archaeology and Christian Liturgy, published in 1903.

This revelation thus invalidated the earlier published claim that the two Latin text parchments said to be discovered in 1891 by Berenger Sauniere, priest of Rennes-Le-Chateau, were written by Abbe Antoine Bigou, priest of Rennes-Le-Chateau, in the 1780's.

Much of the story about Berenger Sauniere, and Rennes-Le-Chateau, and the later Priory of Sion, were revealed to the public by persons associated with the Priory of Sion, who deposited various documents in the National Library of France, and who gave documents to various book authors, from the 1960's to the 1980's.

One of the primary sources of information was the French document known as the Dossiers Secrets, by Henri Lobineau, first made public in 1967. Within the Dossiers Secrets, there are short descriptions of history, and several genealogy charts, including descendants of the ancient Merovingian Kings of France. Many of the genealogies were compiled by Henri Lobineau, in 1956.

Also included in the Dossier Secrets is a document named as Les Descendants Merovingiens, Ou L'Enigme Du Razes Wisigoth, by Madeleine Blancassall. This French document, written soon after 1956, sometime before 1967, contains some details more than the subsequent English language published story of Rennes-Le-Chateau, and Abbe Antoine Bigou, priest of Rennes-Le-Chateau, and Berenger Sauniere, priest of Rennes-Le-Chateau. This author Madeleine Blancassall said that Abbe Antoine Bigou in the 1780's wrote two genealogy manuscripts, the first manuscript being a genealogy, from Merovingian King Dagobert I, to Jean XV Plantard, (b.1548-d.1639). This first genealogy was later reproduced in 1956 by Henri Lobineau, and later by others, including Madeleine Blancassall.

It seems that this first genealogy manuscript by Abbe Antoine Bigou was a combination of the two earlier genealogy parchments, the first parchment dated 1244, bearing the seal of Blanche of Castile, and the second parchment dated 1644, by Francois-Pierre d'Hautpoul, Lord of Rennes-Le-Chateau.

According to Madeleine Blancassall, the second genealogy manuscript by Abbe Antoine Bigou was a genealogy, from Jean XV Plantard, (b.1548-d.1639), to Jean XXI Plantard (b.1784). This second genealogy manuscript has apparently been kept secret, and was not reproduced by Henri Lobineau, and not later by others, including not by Madeleine Blancassall.

Henri Lobineau published a genealogy, from Jean XXI Plantard (b.1784), to Pierre V Plantard, (b.1877-d.1922), who was father of Pierre Plantard, (b.1920-d.2000), who was closely associated with the Priory of Sion, first made public in 1956.

Thus, according to the information from Madeleine Blancassall, it seems that the four parchments, said to have been discovered in 1891 by Berenger Sauniere, priest of Rennes-Le-Chateau, included the first parchment dated 1244, bearing the seal of Blanche of Castile, and the second parchment dated 1644, by Francois-Pierre d'Hautpoul, Lord of Rennes-Le-Chateau, and two genealogy manuscripts written in the 1780's by Abbe Antoine Bigou, priest of Rennes-Le-Chateau.

The first parchment, dated 1244, bearing the seal of Blanche of Castile, has been described as a genealogy, apparently from Merovingian King Dagobert I, to Jean VII Plantard, (b.1204-d.1281), who married in 1244, Elisende De Gisors, (b.1220). Blanche of Castile perhaps attended this 1244 wedding.

The significance of the genealogy parchments and the genealogy manuscripts are the claim or evidence of male line descendants of the Merovingian royal dynasty, previously thought by historians to have become extinct in a strictly male descendant lineage, at the end of the Merovingian dynasty era, at the beginning of the Carolingian dynasty era, but now with genealogy documents of surviving Merovingian male line descendants, particularly in the Plantard family, the Plantard family could claim to be legitimate heirs of the Merovingian royal dynasty in a male lineage, and thus could claim the male lineage right to the royal throne and kingship of France.

Pierre Plantard, (b.1920-d.2000), who was closely associated with the Priory of Sion, first made public in 1956, and who was associated with various book authors who were publicizing the story of Rennes-Le-Chateau and the mystery of Berenger Sauniere and the discovery of parchment genealogies, evidently could claim to be the senior male line representative of the Merovingian royal dynasty, and thus could claim the male lineage right to the royal throne and kingship of France.

The mystery of Berenger Sauniere was the question of how he became wealthy after discovering the parchments.

The following genealogy below, apparently originally from the parchment dated 1244, bearing the seal of Blanche of Castile, and the parchment of 1644, by Francois-Pierre d'Hautpoul, Lord of Rennes-Le-Chateau, is obtained from the Dossiers Secrets documents, genealogies compiled by Henry Lobineau in 1956, apparently from the first genealogy manuscript written by Abbe Antoine Bigou in the 1780's, and the genealogy below is also derived from the genealogy by Madeleine Blancassall, written sometime after 1956, and also partially derived from a later book,

The Priory of Sion, written by Jean-Luc Chaumeil.

The earlier part of the genealogy, to Jean III Plantard (d.c.1070), is reproduced in the book Holy Blood Holy Grail, by Baigent, Leigh, and Lincoln (1982).

In 1979, Pierre Plantard claimed the title, Count of Rhede. In the book, The Priory of Sion, written by Jean-Luc Chaumeil, the last person listed as Count of Rhede was Guillaume II, (d.914).

The title, Count of Rhede, following Guillaume II, are **my** additions.

Most of the estimated dates of birth are my additions.

1. Dagobert I, King of Austrasia, (b.602-d.639).

2. Sigisbert III, King of Austrasia, (b.629-d.656).

3. Dagobert II, King of Austrasia, (b.651-k.679), married (2)(671), Giselle De Razes, (b.653-d.676), daughter of Bera II, Count of Razes.

By this marriage, Dagobert II also became the first Count of Razes of the Merovingian lineage.

4. Sigisbert IV, Count of Razes, (b.676-d.758), married Magdala.

5. Sigisbert V, Count of Razes, (b.c.696-d.c.765).

6. Bera III, Count of Razes, (b.715-d.770), married Olba.

7. Guillaume, Count of Razes, (b.c.735-d.773).

8. Bera IV, Count of Razes, (b.755-d.813), married Romille.

9. Argila, Count of Razes, (b.775-d.836), married Reverge.

10. Bera V, Count of Razes, (b.794-d.860).

11. Hilderic I, Count of Razes and Rhede, (b.c.815-d.867).

12. Sigisbert VI, Count of Razes and Rhede, (b.c.840-d.c.884), married Rotilde, (b.c.843), daughter of Charles II, King of France, (b.823-d.877).

Exiled to Brittany.

13. Guillaume II, Count of Rhede, Duke of Razes, (b.c.857-d.914), married Idoine.

14. Guillaume III Plant-Ard, Count of Rhede, Duke of Razes, (b.874-d.936).

Exiled to England.

15. Arnaud Plant-Ard, Count of Rhede, (b.c.895-d.952).

Returned to Brittany, 939.

16. Bera VI Plant-Ard, Count of Rhede, (b.c.910-d.975).

17. Sigisbert VII Plantard, Count of Rhede, (b.c.930-d.b.982).

18. Hugh I Plantard, Count of Rhede, (b.951-d.971), married Anna.

19. Jean I Plantard, Count of Rhede, (b.c.970-d.1020), married Isabel.

20. Jean II Plantard, Count of Rhede, (b.c.990-d.1054), married Anne.

21. Jean III Plantard, Count of Rhede, (b.c.1010-d.c.1070), married Beatrix of Lorraine, daughter of Gozelon, Duke of Upper Lorraine, (d.1044).

22. Hugh II Plantard, Count of Rhede, (b.c.1030-d.1091).

23. Jean IV Plantard, Count of Rhede, (b.1058-d.1103), Crusader, married Ermende.

24. Pierre I Plantard, Count of Rhede, (b.c.1085-d.1158).

25. Jean V Plantard, Count of Rhede, (b.c.1110-d.1169), married Margueritte Leufroy.

26. Jean VI Plantard, Count of Rhede, (b.1130), married (1156), Idoine De Gisors, (b.1135-d.1191), daughter of Hugh II, Lord of Gisors, (b.1090-d.1142).

27. Louis Plantard, (b.1162-d.1213), younger brother of Pierre II Plantard, Count of Rhede, (b.1160), who married Marguerite, married Guillete De Eix.

28. Louis Plantard, (b.c.1185-fl.1230).

29. Jean VII Plantard, Count of Rhede, (b.1204-d.1281), married (2)(1244), Elisende De Gisors, (b.1220), daughter of Hugh III, Lord of Gisors, (b.1181-d.1225).

30. Jean VIII Plantard, Count of Rhede, (b.c.1250), married Marie Isabel De Veyrac, (b.c.1270)(?).

31. Jean IX Plantard, Count of Rhede, (b.1303), married (1335), Marie Rose De Guildet.

32. Louis I Plantard, Count of Rhede, (b.1341), younger brother of Jean X Plantard, (b.1338-d.1349), married (1385), N.N.

33. Jean XI Plantard, Count of Rhede, (b.1389-d.1446), married (2)(1428), N.N.

34. Jean XII Plantard, Count of Rhede, (b.1430-d.1501), married (1458), N.N.

35. Jean XIII Plantard, Count of Rhede, (b.1460-d.1548), married (2), Marguerite De Biche De Clery.

36. Jean XIV Plantard, Count of Rhede, (b.1514-d.1579), married (1546), Marie De St.Clair-sur-Epte, (b.1530-d.1558), daughter of Robert De St.Clair, (b.1472-d.1538), younger brother of Jacques De St.Clair, Count of St.Clair, (b.1468-d.1551).

37. Jean XV Plantard, Count of Rhede, (b.1548-d.1639).

End of first genealogy manuscript by Abbe Antoine Bigou.

38. Francois I, Count of Rhede, married Claudine, daughter of Hillaire, Lord of Champagne.

The second genealogy manuscript by Abbe Antoine Bigou, from Jean XV Plantard, (b.1548), to Jean XXI Plantard, (b.1784), has been kept secret.

Henri Lobineau, in 1956, wrote the Plantard genealogy, from Jean XXI Plantard, (b.1784), son of Francois III Plantard, to Pierre V Plantard, (b.1877-d.1922).

This genealogy is found within the Dossiers Secrets.

Francois III Plantard, married Benoite Martin.

Jean XXI Plantard (b.1784), married (1808), Marie Clement.

Jean XXII Plantard (b.1809), married (1830), Pierrette Michaud, (b.1810).

Pierre IV Plantard (b.1835-fl.1881), married (1871), Ursule Neant (b.1847).

Elder brother of,

Charles I Plantard (b.1841-fl.1892), married (1877), Elisabeth Julien (b.1849).

Pierre V Plantard , Count of Rhede, (b.1877-d.1922), married (1911), Amelie Raulo.

Henri Lobineau, in this Plantard genealogy of 1956, did not describe the earlier Plantards as Counts of Rhede, but perhaps that was implied. This Plantard genealogy was originally written in 1939 by Abbe Pierre Plantard, (fl.1898-fl.1939), Vicar of the Basilique Sainte Clotilde of Paris.

Pierre V Plantard , Count of Rhede, (b.1877-d.1922), was father of Pierre Plantard (b.1920-d.2000), who married first (1945), Anne Lea Hisler, and he married second (1972), France Germaine Cavaille, and had a son Thomas Plantard, (b.c.1973), and a second child.

Blanche of Castile.

Blanche of Castile, (b.1188-d.1252), married Louis VIII, King of France, (b.1187-d.1226), who were parents of Louis IX, King of France, (b.1215-d.1270).

Blanche of Castile, (b.1188-d.1252), was a younger daughter of Alfonso VIII, King of Castile, (b.1155-d.1214), who married Eleanor of England, (b.1162-d.1214), daughter of Henry II, King of England.

The following pages will give genealogy lines of some ancestors of Blanche of Castile. These genealogy lines below are partially **conjectural**, describing a conjectural descent from ancient Merovingian Kings. Almost all conjectures are **my conjectures.**

Blanche of Castile - Line 1 - Charibert I - Burgundy - Castile

Blanche of Castile - Line 2 - Charibert I - Anjou - Plantagenet

Blanche of Castile - Line 3 - Dagobert I - Asturias - Navarre

Blanche of Castile - Line 4 - Dagobert II - Poitou - Aquitaine

Blanche of Castile - Line 5 - Dagobert II - Barcelona - Castile

Blanche of Castile - Line 6 - Dagobert I - Toulouse

Blanche of Castille - Line 7 - Dagobert I - Navarre - Castile

Blanche of Castille - Line 8 - Dagobert I - Asturias - Leon

Blanche of Castille - Line 9 - Dagobert I - Asturias - Pamplona

Blanche of Castile - Line 10 - Theoderic IV - Autun - Provence

Blanche of Castile - Line 1 - Burgundy - Castile

59. Merovee, King of Franks, (b.c.410-d.457), married N.N.

58. Childeric I, King of Franks, (b.c.436-d.481), married Basina of Thuringia.

57. Clovis I, King of Franks, (b.c.470-d.511), married (492), Clothilda, (b.475-d.548), daughter of Chilperic, King of Burgundy.

56. Chlotar I, King of Franks, (b.c.495/500-d.561), younger son, married (3)(c.520), Ingunde, **perhaps** daughter of Berthar, King of Thuringia, **perhaps** son of Sigebert, King of Cologne.

Reference, Isenburg, Vol. I., Table 1, and RFC Line 303.

55. Charibert I, King of Paris, (b.c.521-d.567), married (4)(c.562), Theodechilde, (b.c.545), **perhaps** daughter of Theodebald, King of Rheims, (b.c.526-d.555), who married (c.545), Waldetrada of Langobards.

Reference, Isenburg, Vol. I., Table 1.

54. Charibert (II) of Neustria, (b.c.566-fl.636), **conjectural younger son of above,** married (c.585), Wulfegunde of Paris, (b.c.565), **perhaps** daughter of Aethelbert I, King of Kent, (b.c.540-d.616), who married (c.560), Audoberta of Paris, (b.c.543), daughter of Charibert I, King of Paris, (b.c.521-d.567), and his first wife Audovera, (b.c.527-div.544).

Reference: RFC Line 169.

53. Chrodobert Robert I of Neustria, (b.c.585-fl.636), married N.N.

Reference, RFC Line 169.

52. Lambert I of Neustria, (b.c.600-fl.650), married (c.615), Sigrada of Orleans, (b.c.600), daughter of Ansaud (b.c.580), who married (c.600), N.N., **perhaps** Gerberge of Orleans, (b.c.585), **probably** daughter of Clothar (II) of Orleans, (b.c.570), who married (c.585), Gerberge of Burgundy, (b.c.570), daughter of Ricomer, Duke of Burgundy. Clothar (II) of Orleans, (b.c.570), was **probably** son of Clothar (I) of Orleans, (b.c.550-d.577), son of Guntram, King of Orleans, (b.c.523-d.592), son of Clothar I, King of Franks, (b.500-d.561), and his third wife, Ingunde,(b.c.505-fl.535), daughter of Berthar, King of Thuringia.

Reference, RFC Line 169 and Line 53.

{conjectural elder son of above, Ancestor of Kings of Castile and Leon. }

51. Guerin Warin Warinus, Count of Poitiers, (b.c.615-d.677), **conjectural elder son of above**, married Gunza of Metz, (b.c.620), daughter of Clodoule, Bishop of Metz, (b.596-d.690).

Reference, RFC Line 53 and Line 330.

50. Liutwin (II), Count and Bishop of Treves, (b.c.640-d.722).

Reference, RFC Line 330.

49. Gui, Count of Treves (?), (b.c.680-fl.722).

Reference, RFC Line 330.

48. Lambert I, Count of Hornbach, younger son, (b.c.720-d.c.783).

Reference, RFC Line 330.

47. Berenger Waringar Warin Werner, Count of Hornbach, younger son, (b.c.760-k.814), married Friderunde.

Reference, RFC Line 200.

46. Berenger, Count of Hornbach, (b.c.775), **conjectural son of above, perhaps** married Willa of Wettergau (?), **perhaps** daughter of Heinrich (I), Count of Wettergau and Saargau, (b.c.755-d.795).

Reference, RFC Line 404.

45. Hunroch Henrich, Margrave of Friuli, (b.c.795-fl.853), married Engeltrude of Paris, (b.c.805), daughter of Eberhard, Count of Paris, (b.c.785).

Reference, RFC Line 404 and Line 332.

44. Amadeus, Count of Burgundy, (b.c.825-fl.872).

Reference, RFC Line 332.

43. Anscar I, Margrave of Ivrea, (b.c.855-fl.891), married Gisele.

Reference, RFC Line 332.

42. Adalbert, Margrave of Ivrea, (b.c.880-d.c.924), married (c.899), Gisele of Italy, (b.c.885-d.913), daughter of Berenger I, King of Italy, (b.850-d.924).

Reference, RFC Line 332 and ES Vol. II., Table 59.

41. Berenger II, King of Italy, (b.c.910-d.966), married (c.935), Willa of Arles and Tuscany, (b.c.920-fl.963), daughter of Boso, Count of Arles and Margrave of Tuscany, (b.c.890-d.936).

Reference, RFC Line 332 and ES Vol. II., Table 59.

40. Adalbert II, King of Lombardy, (b.c.936-d.971), married (c.956), Gerberge of Macon, (b.c.937-d.990), daughter of Lietaud II, Count of Macon, and Richilde of Burgundy.

Reference, RFC Line 94 and ES Vol. II., Table 59.

39. Otto William, Count of Macon and Burgundy, (b.c.958-d.1026), married (972), Ermengarde of Roucy, (b.c.958-d.1005), daughter of Renaud, Count of Roucy, (b.c.926-d.967), who married Alberade of Lorraine, (b.c.930-d.973), daughter of Giselbert, Duke of Lorraine, (b.c.910-d.939), who married (929), Gerberge of Saxony, (b.c.913-d.b.984), daughter of Henry I, King of Germany, (b.c.876-d.936).

38. Renaud I, Count of Burgundy, younger son, (b.c.990-d.1057), married (c.1016), Judith of Normandy, (b.c.1003-fl.1037), daughter of Richard II, Duke of Normandy, (b.c.975-d.1026), who married Judith of Brittany, (b.982-d.1017), daughter of Conan I, Duke of Brittany.

Reference, RFC Line 94 and ES Vol. II., Table 59.

37. William I, Count of Burgundy, (b.c.1024-d.1087), married Stephanie of Longwy, (b.c.1025-fl.1092), daughter of Adalbert III, Duke of Upper Lorraine, (b.c.1010-k.1048).

Reference, RFC Line 94 and ES Vol. II., Table 59.

36. Raymond of Burgundy, younger son, (d.1107), married (c.1095), Urraca, Queen of Castile, (b.1082-d.1126), daughter of Alfonso VI, King of Castile, (b.1039-d.1109), who married (2)(1081), Constance of Burgundy, (d.1092), daughter of Robert I, Duke of Burgundy.

Reference, RFC Line 94 and ES Vol. II., Table 62.

35. Alfonso VII, King of Castile, (b.1105-d.1157), married (1)(1128), Berengaria of Barcelona, (b.c.1116-d.1149), daughter of Raymond Berenger III, Count of Barcelona, (b.1080-d.1131), **Line 5,** who married (3)(1112), Dulce De Gevaudan, (b.c.1095-d.b.1130), daughter of Gilbert, Viscount of Gevaudan, (b.c.1071-d.b.1113), who married (c.1085), Gerberge, (b.c.1071-d.b.1113), **probably** daughter of Raymond IV, Count of Toulouse, (b.c.1045-d.1105), **Line 6,** who married (1066), N.N. of Arles, perhaps Dulce of Arles, (b.c.1045), daughter of Geoffrey I, Count of Arles, (b.c.1010-d.b.1062), who married (c.1033), Dulce of Marseille, daughter of Bertrand, Viscount of Marseille.

Reference, RFC Line 86 and Line 94 and ES Vol. II., Table 62.

34. Sancho III, King of Castile, (b.1134-d.1158), married (1151), Blanche of Navarre, (b.c.1134-d.1156), daughter of Garcia VI, King of Navarre, (b.c.1111-d.1150), **Line 3,** who married (1)(c.1131), Marguerite of L'Aigle, (d.1141), daughter of Gilbert, Lord of L'Aigle, who married Julienne of Perche.

Reference, RFC Line 83 and ES Vol. II., Table 62.

33. Alfonso VIII, King of Castile, (b.1155-d.1214), married Eleanor of England, (b.1162-d.1214), daughter of Henry II, King of England. **Line 2 - Anjou-Plantagenet.**

Reference, RFC Line 83 and ES Vol. II., Table 62.

Blanche of Castile, (b.1188-d.1252), younger daughter.

Reference, ES Vol. II., Table 62.

Blanche of Castile - Line 2 - Anjou - Plantagenet

59. Merovee, King of Franks, (b.c.410-d.457), married N.N.

58. Childeric I, King of Franks, (b.c.436-d.481), married Basina of Thuringia.

57. Clovis I, King of Franks, (b.c.470-d.511), married (492), Clothilda, (b.475-d.548), daughter of Chilperic, King of Burgundy.

56. Clothar I, King of Franks, (b.500-d.561), married (3)(c.520), Ingunde, (b.c.505-fl.535), **perhaps** daughter of Berthar, King of Thuringia, **perhaps** son of Sigibert, King of Cologne.

Reference, Isenburg, Vol. I., Table 1, and RFC Line 303.

55. Charibert I, King of Paris, (b.c.521-d.567), who married (4)(c.562), Theodechilde, (b.c.545), **perhaps** daughter of Theodebald, King of Rheims, (b.c.526-d.555), who married (c.545), Waldetrada of Langobards.

Reference, Isenburg, Vol. I., Table 1.

54. Charibert (II) of Neustria, (b.c.566-fl.636), **conjectural son of above,** married (c.585), Wulfegunde of Paris, (b.c.565), **perhaps** daughter of Aethelbert I, King of Kent, (b.c.540-d.616), who married (c.560), Audoberta of Paris, (b.c.643), daughter of Charibert I, King of Paris, (b.c.521-d.567), and his first wife Audovera, (b.c.527-div.544).

Reference: RFC Line 169.

53. Chrodobert Robert I of Neustria, (b.c.585-fl.636), married N.N.

52. Lambert I of Neustria, (b.c.600-fl.650), married (c.615), Sigrada of Orleans, (b.c.600), daughter of Ansaud (b.c.580), who married

(c.600), N.N., **perhaps** Gerberge of Orleans, (b.c.585), **probably** daughter of Clothar (II) of Orleans, (b.c.570), who married (c.585), Gerberge of Burgundy, (b.c.570), daughter of Ricomer, Duke of Burgundy. Clothar (II) of Orleans, (b.c.570), was **probably** son of Clothar (I) of Orleans, (b.c.550-d.577), son of Guntram, King of Orleans, (b.c.523-d.592), son of Clothar I, King of Franks, (b.500-d.561), and his third wife, Ingunde, (b.c.505-fl.535), daughter of Berthar, King of Thuringia.

Reference: RFC Line 2 and Line 53 and Line 169.

51. Chrodobert Robert II of Neustria, Mayor of Palace of Neustria, (b.c.620-fl.678), married (c.640), Doda, (b.c.620-fl.678), **perhaps** daughter of Dagobert I, King of Neustria and Austrasia and Franks, (b.c.605-d.639).

Reference: RFC Line 169.

50. Lambert (II) of Neustria, (b.c.645), **conjectural generation,** who married N.N., **perhaps** Wandelmode of Poitiers, (b.c.645), **perhaps** daughter of Guerin Warin Warinus, Count of Poitiers, (b.c.615-d.677), who married (c.640), Gunza of Metz, (b.c.620), daughter of Clodoule, Bishop of Metz.

49. Lambert (III), Count of Neustria and Hesbaye, (b.c.670-d.b.741), married (c.685), Chrotlinde of Austrasia, (b.c.672), daughter of Theoderic III, King of Austrasia and Franks, (b.c.656-d.691), who married Chlotilde.

Reference: RFC Line 169.

48. Rudbert Robert, Count of Hesbaye and Wormsgau, (b.689-fl.750), younger second son, who married N.N.

Reference: RFC Line 2 and Line 53 and Line 169.

47. Robert (I), Count of Wormsgau, (b.c.715-d.b.764), married (730), Williswinde of Wormsgau, (b.c.715-fl.768), daughter of Adelhelm Alleaume Guilleaume (II), Count of Wormsgau, (b.c.695-fl.764), who married N.N., **perhaps** Swanhilde (II) of Laon, (b.c.695-d.b.764), **perhaps** daughter of Martin (II) of Laon, (b.c.680), who married (c.695), Bertha of Austrasia, (b.c.680-fl.720), daughter of Theoderic III, King of Austrasia and Franks, (b.c.656-d.691), who married Chlotilde.

Reference: RFC Line 2 and Line 53 and Line 169.

{elder son Ancestor of Robertians and Capets (?)}

46. Guerin, Count of Thurgau, (b.c.735-d.772), younger son, married (c.750), Adelindis, **perhaps** Adelindis of Brittany, (b.c.735), **perhaps** daughter of Meliaw, King of Brittany, (b.c.715-d.792), who married N.N.

Reference, RFC Line 2 and Line 53.

45. Berenger, Count of Thurgau, (b.c.755), **conjectural generation,** married N.N.

44. Bouchard (I) of Thurgau, (b.c.775), married N.N.

43. Aubri I, Count of Fezensac, (b.c.795), married N.N.

Reference, RFC Line 53.

42. Bouchard of Fezensac, (b.c.810), married N.N., **perhaps** Gisele of Maine, (b.c.810), **perhaps** daughter of Rorico Rorigo Rorgon I, Count of Rennes and Maine, (b.c.775-d.c.839), who married (c.800), Bilichilde Bilihilde, (b.c.780), **perhaps** daughter of William (II) of Gellone, Count of Autun and Duke of Toulouse, (b.c.750-d.b.804), who married (1)(c.770), Kunigunde, (b.c.750-fl.804).

41. Geoffrey I, Count of Maine, (b.c.825), **conjectural name,** married N.N., **perhaps** Engeltrude of Orleans, (b.c.825), **perhaps** younger daughter of Eudes Odo Otto, Count of Orleans, (b.798-d.834), who married (c.815), Engeltrude of Paris, (b.c.798-fl.830), daughter of Leutaud, Count of Paris, (b.c.780).

40. Aubri I, Viscount of Orleans, (b.c.840-fl.886), married N.N.

Reference, RFC Line 2.

39. Geoffrey I, Viscount of Orleans, (b.c.855-fl.886), married N.N.

Reference, RFC Line 53.

38. Geoffrey II, Viscount of Orleans, (b.c.870-fl.890), **conjectural generation,** married N.N., **perhaps** Joscelin (b.c.870-fl.890).

37. Geoffrey I, Count of Gatinais, (b.c.890-fl.942), married N.N.

Reference, RFC Line 2.

36. Aubri I, Count of Gatinais, (b.c.910-fl.966), married N.N.

Reference, RFC Line 2 and Line 53.

35. Geoffrey II, Count of Gatinais, (b.c.930-fl.987), married N.N.

Reference, RFC Line 2 and Line 53.

34. Aubri II, Count of Gatinais, (b.c.950-fl.990), married N.N.

Reference, RFC Line 2 and Line 53.

33. Geoffrey III, Count of Gatinais, (b.c.970-fl.990), married Beatrice of Macon, (b.c.970-fl.990), daughter of Aubri III, Count of Macon and Burgundy, (b.c.948-d.b.982), who married (c.969),

Ermentrude of Roucy, (b.c.948-d.1005), daughter of Reginald Renaud, Count of Roucy and Rheims, (b.c.926-d.967), who married (c.948), Alberade of Lorraine, (b.c.930-d.973), daughter of Giselbert, Duke of Lorraine, (b.c.910-d.939), who married (929), Gerberge of Saxony, (b.c.913-d.b.984), daughter of Henry I, King of Germany, (b.c.876-d.936).

Reference, RFC Line 2 and Line 53.

32. Aubri III, Count of Gatinais, (b.c.990- fl.1014), **conjectural generation,** married N.N.

31. Geoffrey IV, Count of Gatinais, (b.c.1014-d.c.1046), married (1035), Ermengarde Blanche of Anjou, (b.c.1018-d.1076), **perhaps** daughter of Geoffrey II, Count of Anjou, (b.c.1006-d.1067), who **perhaps** married (c.1018), Blanche of Auvergne, (b.c.1005-d.b.1032), daughter of Guy Robert, Count of Auvergne, (b.c.985-d.1032), who married (c.1005), Ermengarde of Arles and Provence, (b.c.988), younger daughter of William II, Count of Arles and Provence, (b.c.965-d.c.994), who married Alix Blanche of Anjou, (b.c.965-d.1026), **perhaps** daughter of Geoffrey I, Count of Anjou, (b.c.940-k.987), who married (1)(c.965), Adele of Troyes, (b.c.950-fl.975).

Reference, RFC Line 2 and Line 53 and ES Vol. II., Table 82.

30. Fulk IV, Count of Anjou, (b.1043-d.1109), married (5)(c.1090), Bertrade of Montfort, (b.c.1060-d.1117), daughter of Simon (II) De Montfort, (b.c.1030-d.1087), who married Agnes of Evreux, (b.c.1030), daughter of Richard (II), Count of Evreux, (b.c.1004-d.1067), who married (c.1020), Adelaide De Toeni, (b.c.1004-d.1051), daughter of Roger I De Toeni, (b.c.990-fl.1016), who married (c.1004), Stephanie of Barcelona, (b.c.990-fl.1016), daughter of Raymond Borrell I, Count of Barcelona and Gerona, (b.972-d.1018).

Reference, RFC Line 2 and Line 53 and ES Vol. II., Table 82.

29. Fulk V, Count of Anjou, King of Jerusalem, (b.1092-d.1143), married (1)(1110), Erembourg Ermengarde of Maine, (b.c.1092-d.1126), daughter of Elias Helias, Count of Maine, (b.c.1065-d.1110). Fulk V of Anjou married (2)(1129), Melisende of Rethel, (d.1161), daughter of Baldwin II, King of Jerusalem.

Reference, RFC Line 2 and Line 53 and ES Vol. II., Table 82.

28. Geoffrey V Plantagenet, Count of Anjou, (b.1113-d.1151), married (1128), Matilde of Germany (?), (b.c.1115-d.1167)(?), **probably** daughter of Henry V of Franconia, King of Germany, (b.1081-d.1125), who married (1114), Matilde of England, (b.1102), daughter of Henry I, King of England, (b.c.1070-d.1135), who married (1100), Matilde of Scotland, (b.1079-d.1118), daughter of Malcolm III Canmore, King of Scotland, (b.c.1031-k.1093), who married (2)(c.1068), Margaret Fitz Edward, (b.c.1048-d.1093), daughter of Edward the Aetheling, Prince of England, (b.1016-d.1057), who married (c.1043), Agatha, (b.c.1025-fl.1066), **perhaps** daughter of Heinrich I, Duke of Karnten (?), (b.c.1005-d.b.1047)(?), **perhaps** son of Konrad I, Duke of Karnten, (b.c.990-d.1011), who married (c.1005), Matilde of Swabia, (b.c.988-fl.1011), daughter of Hermann II, Duke of Swabia, (b.c.966-d.1003), who married (c.983), Gerberge of Burgundy, (b.c.966), daughter of Conrad (II), King of Burgundy, (b.c.945-d.993), who married (c.959), Matilde of France, (b.c.943), daughter of Louis IV, King of France, (b.920-d.954).

Reference, RFC Line 2 and Line 53 and ES Vol. II., Table 82.

27. Henry II, King of England, (b.1133-d.1189), married (1152), **perhaps** Eleanor of France, (b.c.1138-d.1204), **perhaps** daughter of Louis VII, King of France, (b.1120-d.1180), who married (1)(1137), Eleanor of Aquitaine, (b.1122-div.1152), daughter of William VIII, Count of Poitou, and Duke of Aquitaine,

(b.1099-1137), who married (1121), Eleanor of Chatellerault, (b.c.1105-fl.1130).

Reference, RFC Line 2 and Line 53 and ES Vol. II., Table 83.

26. Eleanor of England, (b.1162-d.1214), **daughter of above,** married Alfonso VIII, King of Castile, (b.1155-d.1214). **Line 1 - Burgundy-Castile.**

Reference, RFC Line 88 and ES Vol. II., Table 83.

Blanche of Castile, (b.1188-d.1252), younger daughter.

Reference, ES Vol. II., Table 62.

Blanche of Castile - Line 3 - Asturias - Navarre

59. Merovee, King of Franks, (b.c.410-d.457), married N.N.

58. Childeric I, King of Franks, (b.c.436-d.481), married Basina of Thuringia.

57. Clovis I, King of Franks, (b.c.470-d.511), married (492), Clothilda, (b.475-d.548), daughter of Chilperic, King of Burgundy.

56. Chlotar I, King of Franks, (b.c.495/500-d.561), younger son, married (3)(c.520), Ingunde, **perhaps** daughter of Berthar, King of Thuringia, **perhaps** son of Sigebert, King of Cologne.

55. Chilperic I, King of Soissons, (b.c.525-d.584), younger son, married (3)(c.567), Fredegunde, (b.543-d.597).

54. Chlotar II, King of Neustria, (b.c.578-d.629), younger son, married (1)(c.600), Haldetrude Hildetrude, (k.604).

53. Dagobert I, King of Austrasia, King of Franks, (b.602-d.639), married (1)(c.629) Ragnetrude, (2)(c.631) Gometrude, (3)(c.633) Nantilde, (4)(c.635) Wulfegunde, (5)(c.637) Berthilde.

Reference, Isenburg, Vol. I., Table 1, and RFC Line 303.

52. Fruelo, (b.c.636), **conjectural son by Wulfegunde,** married (c.660), N.N., **perhaps** Flavia of Visigoths, (b.c.642), **perhaps** daughter of Fulk, King of Visigoths, (b.c.628-d.642), who married (c.642), N.N., **perhaps** Flavia, (b.c.628), **perhaps** daughter of Ardabast, Prince of Visigoths, (b.c.600), who married N.N., and son of Athanagild, Prince of Visigoths, (b.c.580), who married (c.600), Flavia Juliana of Byzantium, (b.c.580), and son of Hermenagild, King of Visigoths, (b.c.560-k.586), who married (580), Ingunda of Austrasia, (b.c.566-d.585), daughter of **Merovingian** Sigebert I, King of Metz, (b.c.535-k.575), who

married (566), Brunhilde of Visigoths, daughter of Athanagild, King of Visigoths.

Reference, ES Vol. II., Table 48.

51. Favila, Duke of Cantabria, (b.c.660), **conjectural son,** married N.N.

Reference, ES Vol. II., Table 48.

50. Pedro, Duke of Cantabria, (b.c.685), **conjectural younger son,** married (c.710), N.N., **perhaps** Liubigotona of Visigoths, (b.c.690), **perhaps** daughter of Roderigo, King of Visigoths, (b.c.660-d.712), who married (c.680), Egilona, (b.c.662-fl.712), **perhaps** daughter of Egika, King of Visigoths, (b.c.638-d.701), who married (c.660), Cixillo, (b.c.640), daughter of Euric, King of Visigoths, (b.c.620-d.687), who married (c.640), Liubigotona, (b.c.620), daughter of Swinthila, King of Visigoths, (b.c.595-d.633), who married (c.610), Theodora, (b.c.595), daughter of Sigebert, King of Visigoths, (b.c.572-d.620), **perhaps** son of **Merovingian** Sigebert I, King of Metz, (b.c.535-k.575), who married (566), Brunhilde of Visigoths, daughter of Athanagild, King of Visigoths.

Reference, RFC Line 276 and ES Vol. II., Table 49, 48.

49. Alfonso I, King of Asturias, (b.c.710-d.c.757), married (c.730), Hermesinde of Asturias, (b.c.715-fl.748), daughter of Pelayo I, King of Asturias, (b.c.680-d.737), who married (c.705), Gaudiosa, (b.c.685), **perhaps** elder daughter of Roderigo, King of Visigoths, (b.c.660-d.712), who married (c.680), Egilona, (b.c.662-fl.712), **perhaps** daughter of Egika, King of Visigoths, (b.c.638-d.701), who married Cixillo, (b.c.640), daughter of Euric, King of Visigoths, (b.c.620-d.687), who married (c.640), Liubigotona, (b.c.620), daughter of Swinthila, King of Visigoths, (b.c.595-d.633), who married (c.610), Theodora, (b.c.595),

daughter of Sigebert, King of Visigoths, (b.c.572-d.620), **perhaps** son of **Merovingian** Sigebert I, King of Metz, (b.c.535-k.575), who married (566), Brunhilde of Visigoths, daughter of Athanagild, King of Visigoths.

Reference, ES Vol. II., Table 49, 48.

48. Jimeno of Asturias, (b.c.746), **conjectural son of above,** married (c.770), N.N., **perhaps** Galinde of Asturias, (b.c.750), **perhaps** daughter of Inigo of Asturias, (b.c.730), **perhaps** son of Favila, King of Asturias, (b.c.710-d.739), son who married (c.750), N.N., **perhaps** Galinde of Cantabria, (b.c.732), **perhaps** daughter of Fruela, Duke of Cantabria, (b.c.712-d.c.765), who married (1)(c.730), N.N., **perhaps** Galinde of Asturias, (b.c.712-d.b.737), **perhaps** daughter of Pelayo I, King of Asturias, (b.c.680-d.737), who married (c.705), Gaudiosa, (b.c.685), **perhaps** elder daughter of Roderigo, King of Visigoths, (b.c.660-d.712), who married (c.680), Egilona, (b.c.662-fl.712), **perhaps** daughter of Egika, King of Visigoths, (b.c.638-d.701), who married Cixillo, (b.c.640), daughter of Euric, King of Visigoths, (b.c.620-d.687), who married (c.640), Liubigotona, (b.c.620), daughter of Swinthila, King of Visigoths, (b.c.595-d.633), who married (c.610), Theodora, (b.c.595), daughter of Sigebert, King of Visigoths, (b.c.572-d.620), **perhaps** son of **Merovingian** Sigebert I, King of Metz, (b.c.535-k.575), who married (566), Brunhilde of Visigoths, daughter of Athanagild, King of Visigoths.

Reference, RFC Line 223 and ES Vol. II., Table 53, 49, 48.

47. Garcia Jimenez of Asturias, (b.c.775), younger son, who married (c.795), N.N., **perhaps** Oneca, (b.c.775), **perhaps** daughter of Vermudo I, King of Asturias, (b.c.750-d.c.791), who married (c.768), N.N., **perhaps** Munia of Asturias, (b.c.748), **perhaps** daughter of Alfonso I, King of Asturias, (b.c.710-d.c.757), who married (c.730), Hermesinde of Asturias,

(b.c.715-fl.748), daughter of Pelayo I, King of Asturias, (b.c.680-d.737), who married (c.705), Gaudiosa, (b.c.685), **perhaps** elder daughter of Roderigo, King of Visigoths, (b.c.660-d.712), who married (c.680), Egilona, (b.c.662-fl.712), **perhaps** daughter of Egika, King of Visigoths, (b.c.638-d.701), who married Cixillo, (b.c.640), daughter of Euric, King of Visigoths, (b.c.620-d.687), who married (c.640), Liubigotona, (b.c.620), daughter of Swinthila, King of Visigoths, (b.c.595-d.633), who married (c.610), Theodora, (b.c.595), daughter of Sigebert, King of Visigoths, (b.c.572-d.620), **perhaps** son of **Merovingian** Sigebert I, King of Metz, (b.c.535-k.575), who married (566), Brunhilde of Visigoths, daughter of Athanagild, King of Visigoths.

Reference, RFC Line 223 and ES Vol. II., Table 53.

46. Garcia (II) of Asturias, (b.c.800), **conjectural son,** married (c.825), N.N.

45. Jimeno Garcia of Asturias, (b.c.825), married (c.845), N.N., **perhaps** Velasquita of Asturias, (b.c.825), **perhaps** daughter of Ramiro I, King of Asturias, (b.c.790-d.850), who married (1)(c.815), N.N. of Galicia, **perhaps** Bertha of Galicia, (b.c.790-d.b.842), **perhaps** daughter of Alfonso II, King of Asturias and Galicia, (b.765-d.842), who married (c.785), Bertha of Franks, (b.c.765), younger daughter of Pepin III, King of Franks, (b.715-d.768), who married (c.740), Bertha of Laon, (b.c.725-d.783), daughter of Charibert, Count of Laon.

Reference, RFC Line 223 and ES Vol. II., Table 53.

44. Garcia II Jimenez, King of Pamplona, (b.c.845-fl.c.890), married (1)(c.860), Oneca Rebelle of Sanguesa, (b.c.845-d.b.884).

Reference, RFC Line 223 and ES Vol. II., Table 54.

43. Sancho I Garcia, King of Navarre, (b.c.865-d.925), married (2)(c.910), Toda Aznarez of Larron, (b.c.885-fl.970), daughter of Aznar Sanchez of Larron, who married (880), Oneca Fortun of Pamplona, (b.c.847), daughter of Fortun Garcia, King of Pamplona, (b.c.830-d.905).

Reference, RFC Line 223 and ES Vol. II., Table 54.

42. Garcia III Sanchez, King of Navarre, (b.c.913-d.970), married (1), Andregota Galindez, Countess of Aragon, (b.c.919-div.942), daughter of Galindo Aznarez, Count of Aragon.

Reference, RFC Line 223 and ES Vol. II., Table 54.

41. Sancho II, King of Navarre, (b.c.936-d.994), married (962), Urraca Fernandez, (b.935-fl.1007), daughter of Fernando Gonzalez, Count of Castile, (b.c.912-d.970), who married (1)(932), Sancha Sanchez of Navarre, (b.c.915-d.959), daughter of Sancho I, King of Navarre.

Reference, RFC Line 223 and ES Vol. II., Table 55.

40. Garcia IV Sanchez, King of Navarre, (b.c.964-d.999), married (c.980), Jimena Fernandez, (b.c.964-fl.1035), daughter of Fernando Vermudez, (b.c.930-d.978), who married Elvira Diaz, Countess of Saldana, (fl.975).

Reference, RFC Line 223 and ES Vol. II., Table 55.

39. Sancho III, King of Navarre, (b.c.991-k.1035), married (1010), Munia Mayor, Countess of Castile, (b.995-fl.1066), daughter of Sancho Garcia, Count of Castille, (b.c.965-d.1017), who married (994), Urraca Salvadores.

Reference, RFC Line 223 and Line 151 and ES Vol. II., Table 55.

38. Garcia V, King of Navarre, (b.c.1021-k.1054), by **mistress** (c.1038), N.N.

Reference, ES Vol. II., Table 56.

37. Sancho Garcia, (b.c.1040-fl.1073), married (1)(c.1057), Constanza of Maranon, daughter of Sancho Fortun, Lord of Maranon, who married Velasquita.

Reference, ES Vol. II., Table 56.

36. Ramiro Sanchez, Lord of Monzon, (b.c.1070-d.1116), married (c.1100), Christina Elvira Rodriguez, (b.1077-fl.c.1115), daughter of Rodrigo Diaz, "El Cid", Lord of Vivar, (b.c.1043-d.1099), who married (1074), Jimena Diaz, (b.c.1054-d.1115), daughter of Diego, Count of Oviedo, who married Christina Fernandez, daughter of Fernando Gondemarez, who married Jimena of Castile and Leon, daughter of Alfonso V, King of Castile.

Reference, RFC Line 151, 179, 180 and ES Vol. II., Table 56.

35. Garcia VI, King of Navarre, (b.c.1111-d.1150), married (1)(c.1131), Marguerite of L'Aigle, (b.c.1111-d.1141), daughter of Gilbert (II), Lord of L'Aigle, (b.c.1093).

Reference, RFC Line 151 and ES Vol. II.; Table 56.

34. Blanche of Navarre, (b.c.1134-d.1156), **daughter of above,** married (1151), Sancho III, King of Castile, (b.1134-d.1158), **Line 1 - Burgundy-Castile.**

Reference, RFC Line 151 and ES Vol. II., Table 56.

33. Alfonso VIII, King of Castile, (b.1155-d.1214), married
Eleanor of England, (b.1162-d.1214), daughter of Henry II,
King of England, (b.1133-d.1189). **Line 2 - Anjou-Plantagenet.**

Reference, RFC Line 83 and ES Vol. II., Table 62.

Blanche of Castile, (b.1188-d.1252), younger daughter.

Reference, ES Vol. II., Table 62.

Blanche of Castile - Line 4 - Poitou - Aquitaine

59. Merovee, King of Franks, (b.c.410-d.457), married N.N.

58. Childeric I, King of Franks, (b.c.436-d.481), married Basina of Thuringia.

57. Clovis I, King of Franks, (b.c.470-d.511), married (492), Clothilda, (b.475-d.548), daughter of Chilperic, King of Burgundy.

56. Chlotar I, King of Franks, (b.c.495/500-d.561), younger son, married (3)(c.520), Ingunde, **perhaps** daughter of Berthar, King of Thuringia, **perhaps** son of Sigebert, King of Cologne.

55. Chilperic I, King of Soissons, (b.c.525-d.584), younger son, married (3)(c.567), Fredegunde, (b.543-d.597).

54. Chlotar II, King of Neustria, (b.c.578-d.629), younger son, married (1)(c.600), Haldetrude Hildetrude, (k.604).

53. Dagobert I, King of Austrasia, King of Franks, (b.602-d.639), married (1)(c.629) Ragnetrude, (2)(c.631) Gometrude, (3)(c.633) Nantilde, (4)(c.635) Wulfegunde, (5)(c.637) Berthilde.

52. Sigebert III, King of Metz, (b.630-d.656), son of Ragnetrude, married (c.650), Hymnegilde.

Reference, Isenburg, Vol. I., Table 1, and RFC Line 303.

51. Dagobert II, King of Austrasia, (b.651-k.679), married (2)(671), Giselle De Razes, (b.653-d.676), daughter of Bera II, Count of Razes.

Reference, Baigent, Leigh, Lincoln, Holy Blood, Holy Grail.

50. Sigisbert IV, Count of Razes, (b.676-d.758), married Magdala.

49. Sigisbert V, Count of Razes, (b.c.696-d.c.765).

48. Bera III, Count of Razes, (b.715-d.770), married Olba.

47. Guillaume, Count of Razes, (b.c.735-d.773).

46. Bera IV, Count of Razes, (b.755-d.813), married Romille.

45. Argila, Count of Razes, (b.775-d.836), married Reverge.

Reference, Baigent, Leigh, Lincoln, Holy Blood, Holy Grail.

44. Gerard, Count of Auvergne, (b.c.798-k.841), **conjectural younger brother of Bera V, Count of Razes, (b.794-d.860) and Bernard of Razes, Duke of Aquitaine, (b.c.796-k.841)(?).** Married (c.820), N.N., (b.c.800), daughter of Louis I, King of France, Emperor of West, (b.778-d.840), who married (1)(c.794), Ermengarde of Hesbaye,(b.c.778-d.818), daughter of Ingram, Count of Hesbaye.

Reference, RFC Line 163 and ES Vol. II., Table 76

43. Ranulf I, Count of Poitou, and Duke of Aquitaine, (b.820-k.866), married (c.845), N.N., daughter of Rorico, Count of Maine, who married Bilihildis.

Reference, RFC Line 163 and ES Vol. II., Table 76

42. Ranulf II, Count of Poitou, and Duke of Aquitaine, (b.848-d.890), married Ada, (b.c.850-fl.890).

Reference, RFC Line 163 and ES Vol. II., Table 76

41. Ranulf III, Count of Poitou, and Duke of Aquitaine, (b.c.870-d.901), by **mistress** (c.890), Ermengarde, (b.c.870), **perhaps** daughter of Baldwin I, Count of Flanders, (b.c.830-d..879), who married (2)(862), Judith of France, (b.c.844-fl.870), daugter of Charles II, King of France, (b.823-d.877), who married (842), Ermentrude of Orleans, (b.830-d.869).

Reference, ES Vol. II., Table 76

40. Ebles Manzer, Count of Poitou, Count of Auvergne, and Duke of Aquitaine, (b.890-d.934), married (2)(c.911), Emilienne, (b.c.895), **perhaps** daughter of William I, Duke of Aquitaine, (b.c.875-d.918), **Line 10,** who married (c.895), Engelberge of Vienne, (b.c.877-fl.917), daughter of Boso (II), Count of Vienne, King of Provence, (b.c.850-d.887), who married (876), Ermengarde of Italy, (b.c.855-d.896), daughter of Louis II, King of Italy, (b.c.825-d.875), who married (851), Engelberge of Alsace, (b.c.830).

Reference, RFC Line 163 and ES Vol. II., Table 76

39. William I, Count of Poitou, and Duke of Aquitaine, (b.c.915-d.963), married (935), Gerloc Adele of Normandy, (b.c.920-fl.969), **probably** daughter of William I, Duke of Normandy, (b.c.900-k.942), who married (1)(c.920), Sprote of Brittany.

Reference, RFC Line 163 and Line 88 and ES Vol. II., Table 76

38. William II, Count of Poitou, and Duke of Aquitaine, (b.c.937-d.b.996), married (c.968), Emma of Blois, (b.c.950-fl.1003), daughter of Theobald, Count of Blois.

Reference, RFC Line 88 and ES Vol. II., Table 76

37. William III, Count of Poitou, and Duke of Aquitaine, (b.c.969-d.1030), married (3)(1019), Agnes of Burgundy, (b.c.995-d.1068), youngest daughter of Otto William, Count of Burgundy and Macon, and King of Lombardy, (b.c.958-d.1026), **Line 1 - Burgundy - Castile,** who married (1)(c.972), Ermentrude De Roucy, (b.c.958-d.b.1005), daughter of Renaud, Count of Roucy, who married (c.947), Alberade of Hainault and Lorraine, (b.c.930-d.973), daughter of Giselbert, Count of Hainault and Duke of Lorraine, who married (929), Gerberge of Saxony, daughter of Henry I, King of Germany, and Emperor of West.

Reference, RFC Line 88 and ES Vol. II., Table 76

36. William VI, Count of Poitou, and Duke of Aquitaine, (b.c.1024-d.1086), younger son, married (3)(c.1069), Hildegarde of Burgundy, (b.c.1050-d.c.1120), daughter of Robert I, Prince of France, Duke of Burgundy, (b.1011-d.1076), who married (2)(c.1048), Ermengarde Blanche of Anjou, (b.c.1018-d.1076), daughter of Fulk III, Count of Anjou, (d.1040), who married Hildegarde of Metz (d.1046).

Reference, RFC Line 88 and ES Vol. II., Table 76

35. William VII, Count of Poitou, and Duke of Aquitaine, (b.1071-d.1127), married (2)(1094), Philippa Matilde of Toulouse, (b.c.1073-d.1117), daughter of William IV, Count of Toulouse, (b.c.1043-k.1093), **Line 6 - Toulouse,** who married (2)(c.1071), Emma De Mortain, (b.c.1058-fl.1080), daughter of Robert, Count of Mortain.

Reference, RFC Line 88 and ES Vol. II., Table 76

34. William VIII, Count of Poitou, and Duke of Aquitaine, (b.1099-1137), married (1121), Eleanor of Chatellerault, (b.c.1105-fl.1130).

Reference, RFC Line 88 and ES Vol. II., Table 76

33. Eleanor of Aquitaine, (b.1122-div.1152), **daughter of above,** married (1137), Louis VII, King of France, (b.1120-d.1180).

Reference, RFC Line 88 and ES Vol. II., Table 76

32. Eleanor of France, (b.c.1138-d.1204), **perhaps** daughter of above, married (1152), Henry II, King of England, (b.1133-d.1189). **Line 2 - Anjou-Plantagenet.**

Reference, RFC Line 2 and Line 53 and ES Vol. II., Table 83.

31. Eleanor of England, (b.1162-d.1214), married Alfonso VIII, King of Castile, (b.1155-d.1214). **Line 1 - Burgundy-Castile.**

Reference, RFC Line 88 and ES Vol. II., Table 83.

Blanche of Castile, (b.1188-d.1252), younger daughter.

Reference, ES Vol. II., Table 62.

Blanche of Castile - Line 5 - Barcelona - Castile

59. Merovee, King of Franks, (b.c.410-d.457), married N.N.

58. Childeric I, King of Franks, (b.c.436-d.481), married Basina of Thuringia.

57. Clovis I, King of Franks, (b.c.470-d.511), married (492), Clothilda, (b.475-d.548), daughter of Chilperic, King of Burgundy.

56. Chlotar I, King of Franks, (b.c.495/500-d.561), younger son, married (3)(c.520), Ingunde, **perhaps** daughter of Berthar, King of Thuringia, **perhaps** son of Sigebert, King of Cologne.

55. Chilperic I, King of Soissons, (b.c.525-d.584), younger son, married (3)(c.567), Fredegunde, (b.543-d.597).

54. Chlotar II, King of Neustria, (b.c.578-d.629), younger son, married (1)(c.600), Haldetrude Hildetrude, (k.604).

53. Dagobert I, King of Austrasia, King of Franks, (b.602-d.639), married (1)(c.629) Ragnetrude, (2)(c.631) Gometrude, (3)(c.633) Nantilde, (4)(c.635) Wulfegunde, (5)(c.637) Berthilde.

52. Sigebert III, King of Metz, (b.630-d.656), son of Ragnetrude, married (c.650), Hymnegilde.

Reference, Isenburg, Vol. I., Table 1, and RFC Line 303.

51. Dagobert II, King of Austrasia, (b.651-k.679), married (2)(671), Giselle De Razes, (b.653-d.676), daughter of Bera II, Count of Razes.

Reference, Baigent, Leigh, Lincoln, Holy Blood, Holy Grail.

By this marriage, Dagobert II also became the first Count of Razes of the Merovingian lineage.

50. Sigisbert IV, Count of Razes, (b.676-d.758), married Magdala.

49. Sigisbert V, Count of Razes, (b.c.696-d.c.765).

48. Bera III, Count of Razes, (b.715-d.770), married Olba.

47. Guillaume, Count of Razes, (b.c.735-d.773).

Reference, Baigent, Leigh, Lincoln, Holy Blood, Holy Grail.

46. Bello, Count of Carcassonne, (b.c.760-fl.812), **perhaps brother of Bera IV, (b.755-d.813), son of above,** married N.N.

Reference, RFC Line 54 and ES Vol. II., Table 68.

45. Gisclafred, Count of Carcassonne and Razes, (b.c.780-d.821), married (c.810), N.N., **perhaps** Sunigunde, (b.c.785), daughter of Fredelon, who married Aude Bertha of Autun, (b.c.770), daughter of Theoderic (II), Count of Autun, (b.c.750-d.804), who married Aude (d.804).

Reference, ES Vol. II., Table 68 and RFC Line 329.

44. Sunifred I, Count of Barcelona, (b.c.810-d.849), married (c.830), Ermensende, (b.c.810).

Reference, RFC Line 54 and ES Vol. II., Table 68.

43. Sunifred (II), Count of Barcelona, (b.c.835), married N.N.

42. Wilfred I, Count of Barcelona, (b.c.855-d.897), married (877), Guinilde of Flanders, (b.c.863), daughter of Baldwin I, Count of Flanders, (b.c.830-d..879), who married (2)(862), Judith of France,

(b.c.844-fl.870), daugter of Charles II, King of France, (b.823-d.877), who married (842), Ermentrude of Orleans, (b.830-d.869).

Reference, RFC Line 54 and ES Vol. II., Table 68.

41. Wilfred II Borrell, Count of Barcelona, (b.c.880-d.911), married (898), Gersende of Toulouse, (b.c.880), daughter of Eudes (II), Count of Toulouse, (b.c.850), **Line 6 - Toulouse,** who married (c.875), N.N.

Reference, ES Vol. II., Table 68.

40. Suniario I, Count of Barcelona, (b.c.900-d.950), married (2)(c.923), Richilde of Toulouse, (b.c.900-fl.954), daughter of Armengol of Toulouse, Count of Rouergue, younger son, (b.c.877-d.937), who married Adelaide.

Reference, ES Vol. II., Table 68.

39. Borrell I, Count of Barcelona, (b.c.925), married N.N.

38. Borrell II, Count of Barcelona, (b.c.950-d.992), married (1)(968), Luitgarde of Toulouse, (b.c.950-d.c.978), daughter of Raymond III, Count of Toulouse, Count of Auvergne, Duke of Aquitaine, (b.926-fl.961), **Line 6 - Toulouse,** married (c.945), Gersende of Gascony, (b.c.927-fl.975), daughter of Garcia, Count of Gascony.

Reference, RFC Line 54 and ES Vol. II., Table 68.

37. Raymond Borrell I, Count of Barcelona, (b.972-d.1018), married (c.991), Ermensinde of Carcassonne, (b.c.972-d.1057), daughter of Roger I of Comminges, Count of Carcassonne, (b.c.945-d.1019), who married (c.969), Adelaide of Rouergue, (b.c.948-fl.1011).

Reference, RFC Line 54 and ES Vol. II., Table 68.

36. Berenger Raymond I, Count of Barcelona, (b.c.1000-d.1035), married (1021), Sancha of Castile, (b.c.1000-d.1026), younger daughter of Sancho I Garcia, Count of Castile, (b.c.965-d.1017), who married (994), Urraca Salvadores, (b.c.978-d.1025).

Reference, RFC Line 54 and ES Vol. II., Table 69.

35. Raymond Berenger I, Count of Barcelona, (b.1023-d.1076), married (3)(1053), Almode of La Haute Marche, (b.c.1023-k.1071), daughter of Bernard, Count of La Haute Marche, (b.986-d.1047), who married Amelia of Razes.

Reference, RFC Line 54 and ES Vol. II., Table 69.

34. Raymond Berenger II, Count of Barcelona, (b.c.1055-k.1082), married (1078), Matilde of Apulia, (b.c.1058-d.b.1112), daughter of Robert Guiscard De Hauteville, (b.c.1035-d.1085), Duke of Apulia and Calabria and Sicily.

Reference, RFC Line 54 and ES Vol. II., Table 69.

33. Raymond Berenger III, Count of Barcelona, (b.1080-d.1131), married (3)(1112), Dulce De Gevaudan, (b.c.1095-d.b.1130), daughter of Gilbert, Viscount of Gevaudan, (b.c.1071-d.b.1113), who married (c.1085), Gerberge, (b.c.1071-d.b.1113), **probably** daughter of Raymond IV, Count of Toulouse, (b.c.1045-d.1105), who married (1066), N.N. of Arles, perhaps Dulce of Arles, (b.c.1045), daughter of Geoffrey I, Count of Arles, (b.c.1010-d.b.1062), who married (c.1033), Dulce of Marseille, daughter of Bertrand, Viscount of Marseille.

Reference, RFC Line 54 and ES Vol. II., Table 69.

32. Berengaria of Barcelona, (b.c.1116-d.1149), **daughter of above,** married (1128), Alfonso VII, King of Castile, (b.1105-d.1157). **Line 1 - Burgundy-Castile.**

Reference, RFC Line 86 and ES Vol. II., Table 69.

31. Sancho III, King of Castile, (b.1134-d.1158), married (1151), Blanche of Navarre, (b.c.1134-d.1156), daughter of Garcia VI, King of Navarre, (b.c.1111-d.1150), **Line 3 - Asturias-Navarre,** who married (1)(c.1131), Marguerite of L'Aigle, (d.1141), daughter of Gilbert, Lord of L'Aigle, who married Julienne of Perche.

Reference, RFC Line 83 and ES Vol. II., Table 62.

30. Alfonso VIII, King of Castile, (b.1155-d.1214), married Eleanor of England, (b.1162-d.1214), daughter of Henry II, King of England. **Line 2 - Anjou-Plantagenet.**

Reference, RFC Line 83 and ES Vol. II., Table 62.

Blanche of Castile, (b.1188-d.1252), younger daughter.

Reference, ES Vol. II., Table 62.

Blanche of Castile - Line 6 - Toulouse

59. Merovee, King of Franks, (b.c.410-d.457), married N.N.

58. Childeric I, King of Franks, (b.c.436-d.481), married Basina of Thuringia.

57. Clovis I, King of Franks, (b.c.470-d.511), married (492), Clothilda, (b.475-d.548), daughter of Chilperic, King of Burgundy.

56. Chlotar I, King of Franks, (b.c.495/500-d.561), younger son, married (3)(c.520), Ingunde, **perhaps** daughter of Berthar, King of Thuringia, **perhaps** son of Sigebert, King of Cologne.

55. Chilperic I, King of Soissons, (b.c.525-d.584), younger son, married (3)(c.567), Fredegunde, (b.543-d.597).

54. Chlotar II, King of Neustria, (b.c.578-d.629), younger son, married (1)(c.600), Haldetrude Hildetrude, (k.604).

53. Dagobert I, King of Austrasia, King of Franks, (b.602-d.639), married (1)(c.629) Ragnetrude, (2)(c.631) Gometrude, (3)(c.633) Nantilde, (4)(c.635) Wulfegunde, (5)(c.637) Berthilde.

Reference, Isenburg, Vol. I., Table 1, and RFC Line 303.

52. Fruelo, (b.c.636), **conjectural son by Wulfegunde,** married (c.660), N.N., **perhaps** Flavia of Visigoths, (b.c.642), **perhaps** daughter of Fulk, King of Visigoths, (b.c.628-d.642), who married (c.642), N.N., **perhaps** Flavia, (b.c.628), **perhaps** daughter of Ardabast, Prince of Visigoths, (b.c.600), who married N.N., and son of Athanagild, Prince of Visigoths, (b.c.580), who married (c.600), Flavia Juliana of Byzantium, (b.c.580), and son of Hermenagild, King of Visigoths, (b.c.560-k.586), who married (580), Ingunda of Austrasia, (b.c.566-d.585), daughter of **Merovingian** Sigebert I, King of Metz, (b.c.535-k.575), who

married (566), Brunhilde of Visigoths, daughter of Athanagild, King of Visigoths.

Reference, ES Vol. II., Table 48.

51. Favila, Duke of Cantabria, (b.c.660), **conjectural son,** married N.N.

Reference, ES Vol. II., Table 48.

50. Pedro, Duke of Cantabria, (b.c.685), **conjectural younger son,** married N.N., **perhaps** Liubigotona of Visigoths, (b.c.690), **perhaps** younger daughter of Roderigo, King of Visigoths, (b.c.660-d.712), who married (c.680), Egilona, (b.c.662-fl.712), **perhaps** daughter of Egika, King of Visigoths, (b.c.638-d.701), who married Cixillo, (b.c.640), daughter of Euric, King of Visigoths, (b.c.620-d.687), who married (c.640), Liubigotona, (b.c.620), daughter of Swinthila, King of Visigoths, (b.c.595-d.633), who married (c.610), Theodora, (b.c.595), daughter of Sigebert, King of Visigoths, (b.c.572-d.620), **perhaps** son of **Merovingian** Sigebert I, King of Metz, (b.c.535-k.575), who married (566), Brunhilde of Visigoths, daughter of Athanagild, King of Visigoths.

Reference, RFC Line 276 and ES Vol. II., Table 49.

49. Fruela, Duke of Cantabria, (b.c.712-d.c.765), younger son, married (1)(c.730), N.N., **perhaps** Galinde of Asturias, (b.c.712-d.b.737), **perhaps** daughter of Pelayo I, King of Asturias, (b.c.680-d.737), who married (c.705), Gaudiosa, (b.c.685), **perhaps** elder daughter of Roderigo, King of Visigoths, (b.c.660-d.712), who married (c.680), Egilona, (b.c.662-fl.712), **perhaps** daughter of Egika, King of Visigoths, (b.c.638-d.701), who married Cixillo, (b.c.640), daughter of Euric, King of Visigoths, (b.c.620-d.687), who married (c.640), Liubigotona, (b.c.620), daughter of Swinthila, King of Visigoths,

47

(b.c.595-d.633), who married (c.610), Theodora, (b.c.595), daughter of Sigebert, King of Visigoths, (b.c.572-d.620), **perhaps** son of **Merovingian** Sigebert I, King of Metz, (b.c.535-k.575), who married (566), Brunhilde of Visigoths, daughter of Athanagild, King of Visigoths.

Reference, RFC Line 276 and ES Vol. II., Table 49.

48. Aurelio I, King of Asturias, (b.c.730-fl.773), married N.N., **perhaps** cousin Vermuda of Asturias, (b.c.730), **perhaps** daughter of Alfonso I, King of Asturias, (b.c.710-d.757), who married (c.730), Hermesinde of Asturias, (b.c.715-fl.748), daughter of Pelayo I, King of Asturias, (b.c.680-d.737), who married (c.705), Gaudiosa, (b.c.685), **perhaps** elder daughter of Roderigo, King of Visigoths, (b.c.660-d.712), who married (c.680), Egilona, (b.c.662-fl.712), **perhaps** daughter of Egika, King of Visigoths, (b.c.638-d.701), who married Cixillo, (b.c.640), daughter of Euric, King of Visigoths, (b.c.620-d.687), who married (c.640), Liubigotona, (b.c.620), daughter of Swinthila, King of Visigoths, (b.c.595-d.633), who married (c.610), Theodora, (b.c.595), daughter of Sigebert, King of Visigoths, (b.c.572-d.620), **perhaps** son of **Merovingian** Sigebert I, King of Metz, (b.c.535-k.575), who married (566), Brunhilde of Visigoths, daughter of Athanagild, King of Visigoths.

Reference, ES Vol. II., Table 49.

47. Vermudo I, King of Asturias, (b.c.750-d.c.791), married (c.768), N.N., **perhaps** Munia of Asturias, (b.c.748), **perhaps** daughter of Alfonso I, King of Asturias, (b.c.710-d.757), who married (c.730), Hermesinde of Asturias, (b.c.715-fl.748), daughter of Pelayo I, King of Asturias, (b.c.680-d.737), who married (c.705), Gaudiosa, (b.c.685), **perhaps** elder daughter of Roderigo, King of Visigoths, (b.c.660-d.712), who married (c.680), Egilona, (b.c.662-fl.712), **perhaps** daughter of Egika, King of Visigoths, (b.c.638-d.701), who married Cixillo, (b.c.640),

daughter of Euric, King of Visigoths, (b.c.620-d.687), who married (c.640), Liubigotona, (b.c.620), daughter of Swinthila, King of Visigoths, (b.c.595-d.633), who married (c.610), Theodora, (b.c.595), daughter of Sigebert, King of Visigoths, (b.c.572-d.620), **perhaps** son of **Merovingian** Sigebert I, King of Metz, (b.c.535-k.575), who married (566), Brunhilde of Visigoths, daughter of Athanagild, King of Visigoths.

Reference, ES Vol. II., Table 49.

46. Fulk, Count of Rouergue, (b.c.780-d.c.845), **conjectural younger son of above, see Gen. 52.,** married (c.800), Sunigunde, (b.c.785), daughter of Fredelon, who married Aude Bertha of Autun, (b.c.770-fl.804), daughter of Theoderic (II), Count of Autun, (b.c.750-d.804), who married Aude (d.804) .

Reference, RFC Line 329 and ES Vol. III., Table 763.

45. Raymond I, Count of Rouergue and Toulouse, (b.c.805-d.863), younger son, **perhaps grandson of Vermudo I,** married (c.830), Bertha, (b.c.810-fl.883), daughter of Remigius.

Reference, RFC Line 329 and ES Vol. III., Table 763.

44. Eudes (I), Count of Toulouse and Rouergue, (b.c.830), married (c.855), Gersinde of Albi, (b.c.835), daughter of Armengol, Count of Albi, (d.878).

Reference, RFC Line 329 and ES Vol. III., Table 763.

43. Eudes (II), Count of Toulouse and Rouergue, (b.c.855-d.918), married N.N.

42. Raymond II, Count of Toulouse, (b.c.875-d.923), married (c.900), Guinilde of Urgel, (b.c.880-fl.923), daughter of Wilfred, Count of Urgel, (d.897), who married (877), Guinilde of Flanders,

(b.c.863), daughter of Baldwin I, Count of Flanders, (d.879), who married (862), Judith of France, (b.c.844-fl.870), daughter of Charles II, King of France, (b.823-d.877).

Reference, RFC Line 329 and ES Vol. III., Table 763.

41. Raymond Pons, Count of Toulouse, (b.c.900-d.c.932), married (c.925), N.N., **perhaps** Engelberge, (b.c.900), **perhaps** daughter of William I, Duke of Aquitaine, (b.c.875-d.918), **Line 10,** who married (c.895), Engelberge of Vienne, (b.c.877-fl.917), daughter of Boso (II), Count of Vienne, King of Provence, (b.c.850-d.887), who married (876), Ermengarde of Italy, (b.c.855-d.896), daughter of Louis II, King of Italy, (b.c.825-d.875), who married (851), Engelberge of Alsace, (b.c.830).

Reference, ES Vol. III., Table 763.

40. Raymond III, Count of Toulouse, Count of Auvergne, Duke of Aquitaine, (b.926-fl.961), married (c.945), Gersende of Gascony, (b.c.927-fl.975), daughter of Garcia, Count of Gascony.

Reference, RFC Line 329 and ES Vol. III., Table 763.

39. William I, Count of Toulouse, (b.c.947), married (c.975), Arsinde of Anjou, (b.c.950), daughter of Fulk II, Count of Anjou, (b.c.920-d.958), who married (937), Gerberge (d.952).

Reference, ES Vol. III., Table 763.

38. William II, Count of Toulouse, (b.c.975), married (c.1000), N.N., **perhaps** Judith of Bavaria, (b.c.980), **perhaps** younger daughter of Heinrich II, Duke of Bavaria, (b.951-d.995), who married (c.972), Gisele of Burgundy, (d.1006), daughter of Conrad III, King of Burgundy.

Reference, ES Vol. III., Table 763.

37. William III, Count of Toulouse, (b.c.1000-d.1037), married (1019), Emma of Provence, (b.c.1006-d.c.1063), daughter of Roubaud III of Provence, (b.c.980-d.1014), who married (c.1005), Ermengarde, (b.c.985-fl.1016). Roubaud III of Provence, (b.c.980-d.1014), son of Roubaud II, Count of Provence, (b.c.960-d.1008), **probably** son of William I, Count of Arles, (b.c.945-d.978), who married (c.960, N.N. daughter of Aimon of Bourbon. **Line 10 - Autun - Arles - Provence**

Reference, RFC Line 329 and Line 374 and ES Vol. III., Table 763.

36. Pons William, Count of Toulouse, (b.c.1020-d.c.1061), married (2)(c.1041), Almode of La Haute Marche, (b.c.1020-d.b.1078), daughter of Bernard (II), Count of La Haute Marche, (b.c.1000-d.1047).

Reference, RFC Line 374 and ES Vol. III., Table 763.

35. Raymond IV, Count of Toulouse, (b.c.1045-d.1105), younger son, married (1066), N.N. of Arles, **probably** Dulce of Arles, (b.c.1045), daughter of Geoffrey I, Count of Arles, (b.c.1016-d.b.1062), who married (c.1033), Stephanie Dulce of Marseille, daughter of Bertrand, Viscount of Marseille.

Reference, ES Vol. III., Table 764.

34. Gerberge of Arles, (b.c.1071-d.b.1113), **probably daughter of above**, married (c.1085), Gilbert, Viscount of Gevaudan, (b.c.1071-d.b.1113), **probably** younger son of Richard (I), Count of Rodez, (b.c.1050), son of Berenger II, Viscount of Gevaudan, (b.c.1030-d.b.1097), who married (c.1049), Adele of Carlat, (b.c.1030), daughter of Gilbert, Viscount of Carlat.

Reference, RFC Line 257 and ES Vol. III., Table 805.

33. Dulce De Gevaudan, (b.c.1095-d.b.1130), **daughter of above,** married (1112), Raymond Berenger III, Count of Barcelona, (b.1080-d.1131). **Line 5 - Barcelona - Castile.**

Reference, RFC Line 257 and ES Vol. III., Table 805.

32. Berengaria of Barcelona, (b.c.1116-d.1149), **daughter of above,** married (1128), Alfonse VII, King of Castile, (b.1105-d.1157). **Line 1 - Burgundy - Castile.**

Reference, RFC Line 86 and ES Vol. II., Table 69.

31. Sancho III, King of Castile, (b.1134-d.1158), married (1151), Blanche of Navarre, (b.c.1134-d.1156), daughter of Garcia VI, King of Navarre, (b.c.1111-d.1150), **Line 3 - Asturias - Navarre,** who married (1)(c.1131), Marguerite of L'Aigle, (d.1141), daughter of Gilbert, Lord of L'Aigle, who mrried Julienne of Perche.

Reference, RFC Line 83 and ES Vol. II., Table 62.

30. Alfonso VIII, King of Castile, (b.1155-d.1214), married Eleanor of England, (b.1162-d.1214), daughter of Henry II, King of England. **Line 2 - Anjou - Plantagenet.**

Reference, RFC Line 83 and ES Vol. II., Table 62.

Blanche of Castile, (b.1188-d.1252), younger daughter.

Reference, ES Vol. II., Table 62.

Blanche of Castille - Line 7 - Navarre - Castile

Line 7. continues from Line 3.

39. Sancho III, King of Navarre, (b.c.991-k.1035), married (1010), Munia Mayor, Countess of Castile, (b.995-fl.1066), daughter of Sancho Garcia, Count of Castile, (b.c.965-d.1017), who married (994), Urraca Salvadores.

Reference, RFC Line 223 and Line 151 and ES Vol. II., Table 55.

38. Fernando I, King of Castile, (b.c.1017-d.1065), younger son, married (1032), Sancha of Leon, (b.1013-d.1067), daughter of Alfonso V, King of Leon, (b.996-k.1028), **Line 8 - Asturias - Leon,** who married (1)(c.1010), Elvira Menendez, (b.c.996-d.1022), daughter of Menendo Gonzalez, Count of Galicia.

Reference, RFC Line 248 and ES Vol. II., Table 57.

37. Alfonso VI, King of Castile, (b.1039-d.1109), married (2)(1081), Constance of Burgundy, (b.c.1058-d.1092), younger daughter of Robert I, Prince of France, Duke of Burgundy, (b.1011-d.1076), who married (2)(c.1048), Ermengarde Blanche of Anjou, (b.c.1018-d.1076), daughter of Fulk III, Count of Anjou, (d.1040), who married Hildegarde of Metz (d.1046).

Reference, RFC Line 248 and ES Vol. II., Table 57.

36. Urraca, Queen of Castile, (b.1082-d.1126), **daughter of above,** married (c.1095), Raymond of Burgundy, younger son, (d.1107). **Line 1 - Burgundy - Castile.**

Reference, RFC Line 248 and ES Vol. II., Table 57.

35. Alfonso VII, King of Castile, (b.1105-d.1157), married (1)(1128), Berengaria of Barcelona, (b.c.1116-d.1149), daughter of Raymond Berenger III, Count of Barcelona, (b.1080-d.1131), **Line 5 - Barcelona - Castile,** who married (3)(1112), Dulce De Gevaudan, (b.c.1095-d.b.1130), daughter of Gilbert, Viscount of Gevaudan, (b.c.1071-d.b.1113), who married (c.1085), Gerberge, (b.c.1071-d.b.1113), **probably** daughter of Raymond IV, Count of Toulouse, (b.c.1045-d.1105), **Line 6 - Toulouse,** who married (1066), N.N. of Arles, **perhaps** Dulce of Arles, (b.c.1045), daughter of Geoffrey I, Count of Arles, (b.c.1010-d.b.1062), who married (c.1033), Dulce of Marseille, daughter of Bertrand, Viscount of Marseille.

Reference, RFC Line 86 and Line 94 and ES Vol. II., Table 62.

34. Sancho III, King of Castile, (b.1134-d.1158), married (1151), Blanche of Navarre, (b.c.1134-d.1156), daughter of Garcia VI, King of Navarre, (b.c.1111-d.1150), **Line 3 - Asturias - Navarre,** who married (1)(c.1131), Marguerite of L'Aigle, (d.1141), daughter of Gilbert, Lord of L'Aigle, who married Julienne of Perche.

Reference, RFC Line 83 and ES Vol. II., Table 62.

33. Alfonso VIII, King of Castile, (b.1155-d.1214), married Eleanor of England, (b.1162-d.1214), daughter of Henry II, King of England. **Line 2 - Anjou - Plantagenet.**

Reference, RFC Line 83 and ES Vol. II., Table 62.

Blanche of Castile, (b.1188-d.1252), younger daughter.

Reference, ES Vol. II., Table 62.

Blanche of Castille - Line 8 - Asturias - Leon

59. Merovee, King of Franks, (b.c.410-d.457), married N.N.

58. Childeric I, King of Franks, (b.c.436-d.481), married Basina of Thuringia.

57. Clovis I, King of Franks, (b.c.470-d.511), married (492), Clothilda, (b.475-d.548), daughter of Chilperic, King of Burgundy.

56. Chlotar I, King of Franks, (b.c.495/500-d.561), younger son, married (3)(c.520), Ingunde, **perhaps** daughter of Berthar, King of Thuringia, **perhaps** son of Sigebert, King of Cologne.

55. Chilperic I, King of Soissons, (b.c.525-d.584), younger son, married (3)(c.567), Fredegunde, (b.543-d.597).

54. Chlotar II, King of Neustria, (b.c.578-d.629), younger son, married (1)(c.600), Haldetrude Hildetrude, (k.604).

53. Dagobert I, King of Austrasia, King of Franks, (b.602-d.639), married (1)(c.629) Ragnetrude, (2)(c.631) Gometrude, (3)(c.633) Nantilde, (4)(c.635) Wulfegunde, (5)(c.637) Berthilde.

Reference, Isenburg, Vol. I., Table 1, and RFC Line 303.

52. Fruelo, (b.c.636), **conjectural son by Wulfegunde,** married (c.660), N.N., **perhaps** Flavia of Visigoths, (b.c.642), **perhaps** daughter of Fulk, King of Visigoths, (b.c.628-d.642), who married (c.642), N.N., **perhaps** Flavia, (b.c.628), **perhaps** daughter of Ardabast, Prince of Visigoths, (b.c.600), who married N.N., and son of Athanagild, Prince of Visigoths, (b.c.580), who married (c.600), Flavia Juliana of Byzantium, (b.c.580), and son of Hermenagild, King of Visigoths, (b.c.560-k.586), who married (580), Ingunda of Austrasia, (b.c.566-d.585), daughter of **Merovingian** Sigebert I, King of Metz, (b.c.535-k.575), who

married (566), Brunhilde of Visigoths, daughter of Athanagild, King of Visigoths.

Reference, ES Vol. II., Table 48.

51. Favila, Duke of Cantabria, (b.c.660), **conjectural son,** married N.N.

Reference, ES Vol. II., Table 48.

50. Pedro, Duke of Cantabria, (b.c.685), **conjectural younger son,** married N.N., **perhaps** Liubigotona of Visigoths, (b.c.690), **perhaps** younger daughter of Roderigo, King of Visigoths, (b.c.660-d.712), who married (c.680), Egilona, (b.c.662-fl.712), **perhaps** daughter of Egika, King of Visigoths, (b.c.638-d.701), who married Cixillo, (b.c.640), daughter of Euric, King of Visigoths, (b.c.620-d.687), who married (c.640), Liubigotona, (b.c.620), daughter of Swinthila, King of Visigoths, (b.c.595-d.633), who married (c.610), Theodora, (b.c.595), daughter of Sigebert, King of Visigoths, (b.c.572-d.620), **perhaps** son of **Merovingian** Sigebert I, King of Metz, (b.c.535-k.575), who married (566), Brunhilde of Visigoths, daughter of Athanagild, King of Visigoths.

Reference, RFC Line 276 and ES Vol. II., Table 49.

49. Fruela, Duke of Cantabria, (b.c.712-d.c.765), younger son, married (1)(c.730), N.N., **perhaps** Galinde of Asturias, (b.c.712-d.b.737), **perhaps** daughter of Pelayo I, King of Asturias, (b.c.680-d.737), who married (c.705), Gaudiosa, (b.c.685), **perhaps** elder daughter of Roderigo, King of Visigoths, (b.c.660-d.712), who married (c.680), Egilona, (b.c.662-fl.712), **perhaps** daughter of Egika, King of Visigoths, (b.c.638-d.701), who married Cixillo, (b.c.640), daughter of Euric, King of Visigoths, (b.c.620-d.687), who married (c.640), Liubigotona, (b.c.620), daughter of Swinthila, King of Visigoths,

(b.c.595-d.633), who married (c.610), Theodora, (b.c.595), daughter of Sigebert, King of Visigoths, (b.c.572-d.620), **perhaps** son of **Merovingian** Sigebert I, King of Metz, (b.c.535-k.575), who married (566), Brunhilde of Visigoths, daughter of Athanagild, King of Visigoths.

Reference, RFC Line 276 and ES Vol. II., Table 49.

48. Aurelio I, King of Asturias, (b.c.730-fl.773), married N.N., **perhaps** cousin Vermuda of Asturias, (b.c.730), **perhaps** daughter of Alfonso I, King of Asturias, (b.c.710-d.c.757), who married (c.730), Hermesinde of Asturias, (b.c.715-fl.748), daughter of Pelayo I, King of Asturias, (b.c.680-d.737), who married (c.705), Gaudiosa, (b.c.685), **perhaps** elder daughter of Roderigo, King of Visigoths, (b.c.660-d.712), who married (c.680), Egilona, (b.c.662-fl.712), **perhaps** daughter of Egika, King of Visigoths, (b.c.638-d.701), who married Cixillo, (b.c.640), daughter of Euric, King of Visigoths, (b.c.620-d.687), who married (c.640), Liubigotona, (b.c.620), daughter of Swinthila, King of Visigoths, (b.c.595-d.633), who married (c.610), Theodora, (b.c.595), daughter of Sigebert, King of Visigoths, (b.c.572-d.620), **perhaps** son of **Merovingian** Sigebert I, King of Metz, (b.c.535-k.575), who married (566), Brunhilde of Visigoths, daughter of Athanagild, King of Visigoths.

Reference, ES Vol. II., Table 49.

47. Vermudo I, King of Asturias, (b.c.750-d.c.791), married (c.768), N.N., **perhaps** Munia of Asturias, (b.c.748), **perhaps** daughter of Alfonso I, King of Asturias, (b.c.710-d.c.757), who married (c.730), Hermesinde of Asturias, (b.c.715-fl.748), daughter of Pelayo I, King of Asturias, (b.c.680-d.737), who married (c.705), Gaudiosa, (b.c.685), **perhaps** elder daughter of Roderigo, King of Visigoths, (b.c.660-d.712), who married (c.680), Egilona, (b.c.662-fl.712), **perhaps** daughter of Egika, King of Visigoths, (b.c.638-d.701), who married Cixillo, (b.c.640),

daughter of Euric, King of Visigoths, (b.c.620-d.687), who married (c.640), Liubigotona, (b.c.620), daughter of Swinthila, King of Visigoths, (b.c.595-d.633), who married (c.610), Theodora, (b.c.595), daughter of Sigebert, King of Visigoths, (b.c.572-d.620), **perhaps** son of **Merovingian** Sigebert I, King of Metz, (b.c.535-k.575), who married (566), Brunhilde of Visigoths, daughter of Athanagild, King of Visigoths.

Reference, ES Vol. II., Table 49.

46. Vermudo (II), King of Asturias, (b.c.768-d.797), married (c.790), Ursinde Munilona. (b.c.768), **perhaps** daughter of Fruela I, King of Asturias, (b.c.740-d.c.768), who married (c.760), Munia, (b.c.740), **perhaps** daughter of Fruela, Duke of Cantabria, (b.c.712-d.c.765), who **perhaps** married (2)(c.737), Munia of Asturias, (b.c.717), **perhaps** younger daughter of Pelayo I, King of Asturias, (b.c.680-d.737), who married (c.705), Gaudiosa, (b.c.685), **perhaps** elder daughter of Roderigo, King of Visigoths, (b.c.660-d.712), who married (c.680), Egilona, (b.c.662-fl.712), **perhaps** daughter of Egika, King of Visigoths, (b.c.638-d.701), who married Cixillo, (b.c.640), daughter of Euric, King of Visigoths, (b.c.620-d.687), who married (c.640), Liubigotona, (b.c.620), daughter of Swinthila, King of Visigoths, (b.c.595-d.633), who married (c.610), Theodora, (b.c.595), daughter of Sigebert, King of Visigoths, (b.c.572-d.620), **perhaps** son of **Merovingian** Sigebert I, King of Metz, (b.c.535-k.575), who married (566), Brunhilde of Visigoths, daughter of Athanagild, King of Visigoths.

Reference, RFC Line 276 and ES Vol. II., Table 49.

45. Ramiro I, King of Asturias, (b.c.790-d.850), married (1)(c.815), N.N. of Galicia, **perhaps** Bertha of Galicia, (b.c.790-d.b.842), **perhaps** daughter of Alfonso II, King of Asturias and Galicia, (b.765-d.842), who married (c.785), Bertha of Franks, (b.c.765), younger daughter of Pepin III, King of

Franks, (b.715-d.768), who married (c.740), Bertha of Laon, (b.c.725-d.783), daughter of Charibert, Count of Laon.

Reference, RFC Line 276 and ES Vol. II., Table 49.

44. Ordono I, King of Asturias and Galicia, (b.c.820-d.866), married (c.845), Munia, **perhaps** Munia of Pamplona, (b.c.828), **perhaps** daughter of Garcia I Iniguez, King of Pamplona, (b.c.810-d.882), who married (1)(c.828), Urraca (Sancha), (b.c.810-fl.852), **perhaps** Urraca (Sancha) of Asturias, **perhaps** daughter of Ramiro I, King of Asturias, (b.c.790-d.850), who married (1)(c.810), N.N. of Galicia, **perhaps** Bertha of Galicia, (b.c.790-d.b.842), **perhaps** daughter of Alfonso II, King of Asturias and Galicia, (b.765-d.842), who married (c.785), Bertha of Franks, (b.c.765), younger daughter of Pepin III, King of Franks, (b.715-d.768), who married (c.740), Bertha of Laon, (b.c.725-d.783), daughter of Charibert, Count of Laon.

Reference, RFC Line 276 and ES Vol. II., Table 49.

43. Alfonso III, King of Asturias and Galicia and Leon, (b.848-d.910), married (c.870), Jimena Garcia of Pamplona, (b.c.850-d.912), younger daughter of Garcia I Iniguez, King of Pamplona, (b.c.810-d.882), who married (1)(c.828), Urraca (Sancha), (b.c.810-fl.852), **perhaps** Urraca (Sancha) of Asturias, **perhaps** daughter of Ramiro I, King of Asturias, (b.c.790-d.850), who married (1)(c.810), N.N. of Galicia, **perhaps** Bertha of Galicia, (b.c.790-d.b.842), **perhaps** daughter of Alfonso II, King of Asturias and Galicia, (b.765-d.842), who married (c.785), Bertha of Franks, (b.c.765), younger daughter of Pepin III, King of Franks, (b.715-d.768), who married (c.740), Bertha of Laon, (b.c.725-d.783), daughter of Charibert, Count of Laon.

Reference, RFC Line 276 and ES Vol. II., Table 49.

42. Ordono II, King of Asturias and Galicia and Leon, (b.c.873-d.924), married (1)(c.895), Elvira Menendez, (b.c.875-d.921), daughter of Hermenegildo Gutierrez of Portugal, who married Hermesinde Gatonez, daughter of Gaton, Count of Viero, who married Egilona.

Reference, RFC Line 276 and ES Vol. II., Table 49.

41. Ramiro II, King of Leon, (b.c.900-d.951), younger son, married (1)(c.925), Adosinde Gutierrez, (b.c.905-div.930), daughter of Gutierre Osorez, Count of Galicia, (d.c.941).

Reference, RFC Line 276 and ES Vol. II., Table 50.

40. Ordono III, King of Leon, (b.c.926-d.955), by **mistress** (c.949), Aragonta Pelaez, (b.c.930), daughter of Pelayo Gonzalez, (d.c.959), Count of Galicia, who married Hermesende Gutierrez, daughter of Gutierre Menendez.

Reference, RFC Line 276 and ES Vol. II., Table 50.

39. Vermudo II, King of Leon, (b.c.953-d.999), married (2)(991), Elvira Garcia of Castile, (b.c.970-d.1017), daughter of Garcia I Fernandez, Count of Castile, (b.c.940-d.995), who married (c.960), Aba (Ava) of Ribagorza, (b.c.940-fl.995), daughter of Ramon, Count of Ribagorza.

Reference, RFC Line 276 and ES Vol. II., Table 50.

38. Alfonso V, King of Leon, (b.996-k.1028), married (1)(c.1010), Elvira Menendez, (b.c.996-d.1022), daughter of Menendo Gonzalez, Count of Galicia.

Reference, RFC Line 276 and ES Vol. II., Table 50.

37. Sancha of Leon, (b.1013-d.1067), **daughter of above,** married (1032), Fernando I, King of Castile, (b.c.1017-d.1065).
Line 7 - Navarre - Castile.

Reference, RFC Line 276 and ES Vol. II., Table 50.

36. Alfonso VI, King of Castile, (b.1039-d.1109), married (2)(1081), Constance of Burgundy, (b.c.1058-d.1092), younger daughter of Robert I, Prince of France, Duke of Burgundy, (b.1011-d.1076), who married (2)(c.1048), Ermengarde Blanche of Anjou, (b.c.1018-d.1076), daughter of Fulk III, Count of Anjou, (d.1040), who married Hildegarde of Metz (d.1046).

Reference, RFC Line 248 and ES Vol. II., Table 57.

35. Urraca, Queen of Castile, (b.1082-d.1126), **daughter of above,** married (c.1095), Raymond of Burgundy, younger son, (d.1107).
Line 1 - Burgundy - Castile.

Reference, RFC Line 248 and ES Vol. II., Table 57.

34. Alfonso VII, King of Castile, (b.1105-d.1157), married (1)(1128), Berengaria of Barcelona, (b.c.1116-d.1149), daughter of Raymond Berenger III, Count of Barcelona, (b.1080-d.1131), **Line 5 - Barcelona - Castile,** who married (3)(1112), Dulce De Gevaudan, (b.c.1095-d.b.1130), daughter of Gilbert, Viscount of Gevaudan, (b.c.1071-d.b.1113), who married (c.1085), Gerberge, (b.c.1071-d.b.1113), **probably** daughter of Raymond IV, Count of Toulouse, (b.c.1045-d.1105), **Line 6 - Toulouse,** who married (1066), N.N. of Arles, perhaps Dulce of Arles, (b.c.1045), daughter of Geoffrey I, Count of Arles, (b.c.1010-d.b.1062), who married (c.1033), Dulce of Marseille, daughter of Bertrand, Viscount of Marseille.

Reference, RFC Line 86 and Line 94 and ES Vol. II., Table 62.

33. Sancho III, King of Castile, (b.1134-d.1158), married (1151), Blanche of Navarre, (b.c.1134-d.1156), daughter of Garcia VI, King of Navarre, (b.c.1111-d.1150), **Line 3 - Asturias - Navarre,** who married (1)(c.1131), Marguerite of L'Aigle, (d.1141), daughter of Gilbert, Lord of L'Aigle, who married Julienne of Perche.

Reference, RFC Line 83 and ES Vol. II., Table 62.

32. Alfonso VIII, King of Castile, (b.1155-d.1214), married Eleanor of England, (b.1162-d.1214), daughter of Henry II, King of England. **Line 2 - Anjou - Plantagenet.**

Reference, RFC Line 83 and ES Vol. II., Table 62.

Blanche of Castile, (b.1188-d.1252), younger daughter.

Reference, ES Vol. II., Table 62.

Blanche of Castile - Line 9 - Asturias - Pamplona

59. Merovee, King of Franks, (b.c.410-d.457), married N.N.

58. Childeric I, King of Franks, (b.c.436-d.481), married Basina of Thuringia.

57. Clovis I, King of Franks, (b.c.470-d.511), married (492), Clothilda, (b.475-d.548), daughter of Chilperic, King of Burgundy.

56. Chlotar I, King of Franks, (b.c.495/500-d.561), younger son, married (3)(c.520), Ingunde, **perhaps** daughter of Berthar, King of Thuringia, **perhaps** son of Sigebert, King of Cologne.

55. Chilperic I, King of Soissons, (b.c.525-d.584), younger son, married (3)(c.567), Fredegunde, (b.543-d.597).

54. Chlotar II, King of Neustria, (b.c.578-d.629), younger son, married (1)(c.600), Haldetrude Hildetrude, (k.604).

53. Dagobert I, King of Austrasia, King of Franks, (b.602-d.639), married (1)(c.629) Ragnetrude, (2)(c.631) Gometrude, (3)(c.633) Nantilde, (4)(c.635) Wulfegunde, (5)(c.637) Berthilde.

Reference, Isenburg, Vol. I., Table 1, and RFC Line 303.

52. Fruelo, (b.c.636), **conjectural son by Wulfegunde,** married (c.660), N.N., **perhaps** Flavia of Visigoths, (b.c.642), **perhaps** daughter of Fulk, King of Visigoths, (b.c.628-d.642), who married (c.642), N.N., **perhaps** Flavia, (b.c.628), **perhaps** daughter of Ardabast, Prince of Visigoths, (b.c.600), who married N.N., and son of Athanagild, Prince of Visigoths, (b.c.580), who married (c.600), Flavia Juliana of Byzantium, (b.c.580), and son of Hermenagild, King of Visigoths, (b.c.560-k.586), who married (580), Ingunda of Austrasia, (b.c.566-d.585), daughter of **Merovingian** Sigebert I, King of Metz, (b.c.535-k.575), who

married (566), Brunhilde of Visigoths, daughter of Athanagild, King of Visigoths.

Reference, ES Vol. II., Table 48.

51. Favila, Duke of Cantabria, (b.c.660), **conjectural son,** married N.N.

Reference, ES Vol. II., Table 48.

50. Pedro, Duke of Cantabria, (b.c.685), **conjectural younger son,** married (c.710), N.N., **perhaps** Liubigotona of Visigoths, (b.c.690), **perhaps** daughter of Roderigo, King of Visigoths, (b.c.660-d.712), who married (c.680), Egilona, (b.c.662-fl.712), **perhaps** daughter of Egika, King of Visigoths, (b.c.638-d.701), who married (c.660), Cixillo, (b.c.640), daughter of Euric, King of Visigoths, (b.c.620-d.687), who married (c.640), Liubigotona, (b.c.620), daughter of Swinthila, King of Visigoths, (b.c.595-d.633), who married (c.610), Theodora, (b.c.595), daughter of Sigebert, King of Visigoths, (b.c.572-d.620), **perhaps** son of **Merovingian** Sigebert I, King of Metz, (b.c.535-k.575), who married (566), Brunhilde of Visigoths, daughter of Athanagild, King of Visigoths.

Reference, RFC Line 276 and ES Vol. II., Table 49, 48.

49. Alfonso I, King of Asturias, (b.c.710-d.c.757), married (c.730), Hermesinde of Asturias, (b.c.715-fl.748), daughter of Pelayo I, King of Asturias, (b.c.680-d.737), who married (c.705), Gaudiosa, (b.c.685), **perhaps** elder daughter of Roderigo, King of Visigoths, (b.c.660-d.712), who married (c.680), Egilona, (b.c.662-fl.712), **perhaps** daughter of Egika, King of Visigoths, (b.c.638-d.701), who married Cixillo, (b.c.640), daughter of Euric, King of Visigoths, (b.c.620-d.687), who married (c.640), Liubigotona, (b.c.620), daughter of Swinthila, King of Visigoths, (b.c.595-d.633), who married (c.610), Theodora, (b.c.595),

daughter of Sigebert, King of Visigoths, (b.c.572-d.620), **perhaps** son of **Merovingian** Sigebert I, King of Metz, (b.c.535-k.575), who married (566), Brunhilde of Visigoths, daughter of Athanagild, King of Visigoths.

Reference, ES Vol. II., Table 49, 48.

48. Jimeno of Asturias, (b.c.746), **conjectural son of above,** married (c.770), N.N., **perhaps** Galinde of Asturias, (b.c.750), **perhaps** daughter of Inigo of Asturias, (b.c.730), **perhaps** son of Favila, King of Asturias, (b.c.710-d.739), and who married (c.750), N.N., **perhaps** Galinde of Cantabria, (b.c.732), **perhaps** daughter of Fruela, Duke of Cantabria, (b.c.712-d.c.765), who married (1)(c.730), N.N., **perhaps** Galinde of Asturias, (b.c.712-d.b.737), **perhaps** daughter of Pelayo I, King of Asturias, (b.c.680-d.737), who married (c.705), Gaudiosa, (b.c.685), **perhaps** elder daughter of Roderigo, King of Visigoths, (b.c.660-d.712), who married (c.680), Egilona, (b.c.662-fl.712), **perhaps** daughter of Egika, King of Visigoths, (b.c.638-d.701), who married Cixillo, (b.c.640), daughter of Euric, King of Visigoths, (b.c.620-d.687), who married (c.640), Liubigotona, (b.c.620), daughter of Swinthila, King of Visigoths, (b.c.595-d.633), who married (c.610), Theodora, (b.c.595), daughter of Sigebert, King of Visigoths, (b.c.572-d.620), **perhaps** son of **Merovingian** Sigebert I, King of Metz, (b.c.535-k.575), who married (566), Brunhilde of Visigoths, daughter of Athanagild, King of Visigoths.

Reference, RFC Line 76 and ES Vol. II., Table 53.

46. Inigo Jimenez, (b.c.770), married (2)(c.790), N.N., **probably** sister of Musa Ibn Fortun, Chief of the Banu Qasi family, and **probably** daughter of Fortun, Chief of the Banu Qasi family.

Reference, RFC Line 76 and ES Vol. II., Table 53.

45. Inigo Iniguez, King of Pamplona, (b.c.790-d.b.852), married (c.810), Oneca, (b.c.795), **perhaps** daughter of Garcia Jimenez of Asturias, (b.c.775), who married (c.795), N.N., **perhaps** Oneca, (b.c.775), **perhaps** daughter of Vermudo I, King of Asturias, (b.c.750-d.c.791), married (c.768), N.N., **perhaps** Munia of Asturias, (b.c.748), **perhaps** daughter of Alfonso I, King of Asturias, (b.c.710-d.c.757), who married (c.730), Hermesinde of Asturias, (b.c.715-fl.748), daughter of Pelayo I, King of Asturias, (b.c.680-d.737), who married (c.705), Gaudiosa, (b.c.685), **perhaps** elder daughter of Roderigo, King of Visigoths, (b.c.660-d.712), who married (c.680), Egilona, (b.c.662-fl.712), **perhaps** daughter of Egika, King of Visigoths, (b.c.638-d.701), who married Cixillo, (b.c.640), daughter of Euric, King of Visigoths, (b.c.620-d.687), who married (c.640), Liubigotona, (b.c.620), daughter of Swinthila, King of Visigoths, (b.c.595-d.633), who married (c.610), Theodora, (b.c.595), daughter of Sigebert, King of Visigoths, (b.c.572-d.620), **perhaps** son of **Merovingian** Sigebert I, King of Metz, (b.c.535-k.575), who married (566), Brunhilde of Visigoths, daughter of Athanagild, King of Visigoths.

Reference, RFC Line 76 and ES Vol. II., Table 53.

44. Garcia I Iniguez, King of Pamplona, (b.c.810-d.882), married (1)(c.828), Urraca (Sancha), (b.c.810-fl.852), **perhaps** Urraca (Sancha) of Asturias, **perhaps** daughter of Ramiro I, King of Asturias, (b.c.790-d.850), who married (1)(c.810), N.N. of Galicia, **perhaps** Bertha of Galicia, (b.c.790-d.b.842), **perhaps** daughter of Alfonso II, King of Asturias and Galicia, (b.765-d.842), who married (c.785), Bertha of Franks, (b.c.765), younger daughter of Pepin III, King of Franks, (b.715-d.768), who married (c.740), Bertha of Laon, (b.c.725-d.783), daughter of Charibert, Count of Laon.

Reference, RFC Line 76 and ES Vol. II., Table 53.

43. Jimena Garcia of Pamplona, (b.c.850-d.912), **younger daughter of above**, married (c.870), Alfonso III, King of Asturias and Galicia and Leon, (b.848-d.910). **Line 8 - Asturias - Leon**

Reference, RFC Line 76 and ES Vol. II., Table 53.

42. Ordono II, King of Asturias and Galicia and Leon, (b.c.873-d.924), married (1)(c.895), Elvira Menendez, (b.c.875-d.921), daughter of Hermenegildo Gutierrez of Portugal, who married Hermesinde Gatonez, daughter of Gaton, Count of Viero, who married Egilona.

Reference, RFC Line 276 and ES Vol. II., Table 49.

41. Ramiro II, King of Leon, (b.c.900-d.951), younger son, married (1)(c.925), Adosinde Gutierrez, (b.c.905-div.930), daughter of Gutierre Osorez, Count of Galicia, (d.c.941).

Reference, RFC Line 276 and ES Vol. II., Table 50.

40. Ordono III, King of Leon, (b.c.926-d.955), by **mistress** (c.949), Aragonta Pelaez, (b.c.930), daughter of Pelayo Gonzalez, (d.c.959), Count of Galicia, who married Hermesende Gutierrez, daughter of Gutierre Menendez.

Reference, RFC Line 276 and ES Vol. II., Table 50.

39. Vermudo II, King of Leon, (b.c.953-d.999), married (2)(991), Elvira Garcia of Castile, (b.c.970-d.1017), daughter of Garcia I Fernandez, Count of Castile, (b.c.940-d.995), who married (c.960), Aba (Ava) of Ribagorza, (b.c.940-fl.995), daughter of Ramon, Count of Ribagorza.

Reference, RFC Line 276 and ES Vol. II., Table 50.

38. Alfonso V, King of Leon, (b.996-k.1028), married (1)(c.1010), Elvira Menendez, (b.c.996-d.1022), daughter of Menendo Gonzalez, Count of Galicia.

Reference, RFC Line 276 and ES Vol. II., Table 50.

37. Sancha of Leon, (b.1013-d.1067), **daughter of above,** married (1032), Fernando I, King of Castile, (b.c.1017-d.1065). **Line 7 - Navarre - Castile.**

Reference, RFC Line 276 and ES Vol. II., Table 50.

36. Alfonso VI, King of Castile, (b.1039-d.1109), married (2)(1081), Constance of Burgundy, (b.c.1058-d.1092), younger daughter of Robert I, Prince of France, Duke of Burgundy, (b.1011-d.1076), who married (2)(c.1048), Ermengarde Blanche of Anjou, (b.c.1018-d.1076), daughter of Fulk III, Count of Anjou, (d.1040), who married Hildegarde of Metz (d.1046).

Reference, RFC Line 248 and ES Vol. II., Table 57.

35. Urraca, Queen of Castile, (b.1082-d.1126), **daughter of above,** married (c.1095), Raymond of Burgundy, younger son, (d.1107). **Line 1 - Burgundy - Castile.**

Reference, RFC Line 248 and ES Vol. II., Table 57.

34. Alfonso VII, King of Castile, (b.1105-d.1157), married (1)(1128), Berengaria of Barcelona, (b.c.1116-d.1149), daughter of Raymond Berenger III, Count of Barcelona, (b.1080-d.1131), **Line 5 - Barcelona - Castile,** who married (3)(1112), Dulce De Gevaudan, (b.c.1095-d.b.1130), daughter of Gilbert, Viscount of Gevaudan, (b.c.1071-d.b.1113), who married (c.1085), Gerberge, (b.c.1071-d.b.1113), **probably** daughter of Raymond IV, Count of Toulouse, (b.c.1045-d.1105), **Line 6 - Toulouse,** who married (1066), N.N. of Arles, perhaps Dulce of Arles, (b.c.1045),

daughter of Geoffrey I, Count of Arles, (b.c.1010-d.b.1062), who married (c.1033), Dulce of Marseille, daughter of Bertrand, Viscount of Marseille.

Reference, RFC Line 86 and Line 94 and ES Vol. II., Table 62.

33. Sancho III, King of Castile, (b.1134-d.1158), married (1151), Blanche of Navarre, (b.c.1134-d.1156), daughter of Garcia VI, King of Navarre, (b.c.1111-d.1150), **Line 3 - Asturias - Navarre,** who married (1)(c.1131), Marguerite of L'Aigle, (d.1141), daughter of Gilbert, Lord of L'Aigle, who married Julienne of Perche.

Reference, RFC Line 83 and ES Vol. II., Table 62.

32. Alfonso VIII, King of Castile, (b.1155-d.1214), married Eleanor of England, (b.1162-d.1214), daughter of Henry II, King of England. **Line 2 - Anjou - Plantagenet.**

Reference, RFC Line 83 and ES Vol. II., Table 62.

Blanche of Castile, (b.1188-d.1252), younger daughter.

Reference, ES Vol. II., Table 62.

Blanche of Castile - Line 10 - Autun - Arles - Provence

59. Merovee, King of Franks, (b.c.410-d.457), married N.N.

58. Childeric I, King of Franks, (b.c.436-d.481), married Basina of Thuringia.

57. Clovis I, King of Franks, (b.c.470-d.511), married (492), Clothilda, (b.475-d.548), daughter of Chilperic, King of Burgundy.

56. Chlotar I, King of Franks, (b.c.495/500-d.561), younger son, married (3)(c.520), Ingunde, **perhaps** daughter of Berthar, King of Thuringia, **perhaps** son of Sigebert, King of Cologne.

55. Chilperic I, King of Soissons, (b.c.525-d.584), younger son, married (3)(c.567), Fredegunde, (b.543-d.597).

54. Chlotar II, King of Neustria, (b.c.578-d.629), younger son, married (1)(c.600), Haldetrude Hildetrude, (k.604).

Reference, Isenburg, Vol. I., Table 1, and RFC Line 303

53. Dagobert I, King of Austrasia, King of Franks, (b.602-d.639), married (1)(c.629) Ragnetrude, (2)(c.631) Gometrude, (3)(c.633) Nantilde, (4)(c.635) Wulfegunde, (5)(c.637) Berthilde.

Reference, Isenburg, Vol. I., Table 1, and RFC Line 303 and 123

52. Clovis II, King of Neustria and Franks, (b.634-d.657), younger son, son of Nantilde, married (c.653), Bathilde (d.680).

Reference, Isenburg, Vol. I., Table 1, and RFC Line 123.

51. Theoderic III, King of Austrasia and Franks, (b.c.656-d.691), younger son, married (c.671), Chlotilde.

Reference, Isenburg, Vol. I., Table 1, and RFC Line 123.

50. Childebert III, King of Austrasia and Franks, (b.674-d.711), younger son, married N.N. .

49. Dagobert III, King of Austrasia and Franks, (b.689-d.715), married N.N.

48. Theoderic IV, King of Austrasia, (b.c.705-d.737), married N.N.

Reference, Isenburg, Vol. I., Table 1.

47. Theoderic (I), Count of Autun, Duke of Toulouse, (b.c.725-d.c.782), **perhaps son of above,** married (1)(c.743), Aude of Austrasia, (b.c.722-d.804), daughter of Carloman, Mayor of Palace of Austrasia, (b.c.695-d.754), son of Charles Martel, King of Franks, (b.c.674-d.741).

Reference, RFC Line 326 and ES Vol. III., Table 731.

46. William of Gellone, Count of Autun, Duke of Toulouse, (b.c.745-d.b.804), married (c.770), Kunigunde, (b.c.755-fl.804), **probably** sister of Charlemagne, King of France (b.747-d.814), and daughter of Pepin III, King of Franks, (b.715-d.768), who married (c.740), Bertha Bertrade of Laon, (b.c.720-d.783), daughter of Charibert (Heribert), Count of Laon, (b.c.695-fl.747).

Reference, RFC Line 326 and ES Vol. III., Table 731.

45. William (II) of Gellone, Count of Autun, Duke of Toulouse, (b.c.770-d.b.815), married (c.785), Guitburge of Hornbach, (b.c.770-fl.804), daughter of Lambert (III), Count of Hornbach.

Reference, RFC Line 326 and ES Vol. III., Table 731.

44. Bernard, Count of Autun, Margrave of Septimania, (b.795-k.844), married (824), Dhoude, (b.c.805-fl.843), younger half-sister of Louis I, King of France, (b.778-d.840), sister of Aribert (Heribert), (b.c.800), daughter of Charlemagne, King of France, (b.747-d.814), who married (8)(c.795), Regina Adelinde.

Reference, RFC Line 326 and ES Vol. III., Table 731.

43. Bernard (II), Count of Autun, Count of Auvergne, (b.841-d.b.886), younger son, married (c.870), Ermengarde, daughter of Count Bernard I, who married Liutgarde, **probably** Ermengarde of Toulouse, (b.c.850-fl.881), daughter of Bernard I, Count of Toulouse, (b.c.825-d.874), who **probably** married Liutgarde.

Reference, ES Vol. III., Table 731.

42. William I, Duke of Aquitaine, (b.c.875-d.918), married (c.895), Engelberge of Vienne, (b.c.877-fl.917), daughter of Boso (II), Count of Vienne, King of Provence, (b.c.850-d.887), who married (876), Ermengarde of Italy, (b.c.855-d.896), daughter of Louis II, King of Italy, (b.c.825-d.875), who married (851), Engelberge of Alsace, (b.c.830).

Reference, ES Vol. III., Table 731.

41. Ermengarde of Aquitaine, (b.c.905), **daughter of above,** married (c.925), Roubaud I of Agel, (b.c.890-d.949), **perhaps** younger son of Theobald, Count of Arles and Vienne, (b.c.860-d.c.895), who married (c.880), Bertha of Lorraine, (b.c.863-d.925), daughter of Lothar II, King of Lorraine (d.869).

Reference, ES Vol. III., Table 731.

40. Boso II, Count of Arles, (b.928-d.b.967), married (c.945), Constance of Provence, (b.c.928-d.b.965), daughter of Charles

Constantine, Count of Vienne, (b.c.901-fl.962), who married (c.920), Teutberge of Arles and Vienne, (b.c.895-d.948), daughter of Theobald, Count of Arles and Vienne, (b.c.860-d.c.895), who married (c.880), Bertha of Lorraine, (b.c.863-d.925), daughter of Lothar II, King of Lorraine (d.869).

Reference, RFC Line 333 and ES Vol. II., Table 187.

39. William I, Count of Arles, (b.c.945-d.c.978), married (c.960), N.N., daughter of Aimon of Bourbon.

Reference, ES Vol. II., Table 187.

38. William II, Count of Arles and Provence, (b.c.962-d.994), **probably younger son of above,** married (2)(c.984), Adelaide Blanche of Anjou, (b.c.962-d.1026), **probably** daughter of Geoffrey I, Count of Anjou, (b.c.940-k.987), who married (c.960), Adele of Vermandois and Troyes, (b.c.940-d.b.978).

Reference, RFC Line 333 and Line 298 and ES Vol. II., Table 187.

37. William III, Count of Provence, (b.c.984-d.1018), married (c.1002), Gerberge of Burgundy, (b.c.985-d.b.1023), daughter of Otto William, Count of Macon and Burgundy, King of Lombardy, (b.c.958-d.1026), **Line 1 - Burgundy - Castile,** who married (1)(c.982), Ermentrude of Roucy, (b.958-d.b.1005), daughter of Renaud, Count of Roucy, (b.c.926-d.967), who married (c.944), Alberade of Lorraine, (b.c.930-d.973), daughter of Giselbert, Duke of Lorraine.

Reference, RFC Line 298 and ES Vol. II., Table 187.

36. William IV, Count of Provence, (b.c.1002-d.b.1030), married, (c.1016), Adele of Anjou (b.c.1002-d.1029), daughter of Fulk III, Count of Anjou, (b.967-d.1040), who married (2)(c.1000), Hildegarde of Metz, (b.c.985-d.1046), daughter of Folmar II,

Count of Metz, (b.c.960-d.b.1029), who married (c.985), Gerberge of Verdun, (b.c.965), daughter of Godfrey, Count of Verdun, (b.c.935-fl.1005).

Reference, ES Vol. II., Table 187.

35. Geoffrey I, Count of Arles, (b.c.1018-d.b.1062), younger son, who married (c.1033), Stephanie Dulce of Marseille, daughter of Bertrand, Viscount of Marseille.

Reference, RFC Line 298 and ES Vol. II., Table 187.

34. Dulce of Arles, (b.c.1045), **daughter of above,** married (1066), Raymond IV, Count of Toulouse, (b.c.1045-d.1105). **Line 6 - Toulouse**

Reference, RFC Line 298 and ES Vol. II., Table 187.

33. Gerberge of Arles, (b.c.1071-d.b.1113), **probably daughter of above**, married (c.1085), Gilbert, Viscount of Gevaudan, (b.c.1071-d.b.1113), **probably** younger son of Richard (I), Count of Rodez, (b.c.1050), son of Berenger II, Viscount of Gevaudan, (b.c.1030-d.b.1097), who married (c.1049), Adele of Carlat, (b.c.1030), daughter of Gilbert, Viscount of Carlat.

Reference, RFC Line 298 and Line 257 and ES Vol. III., Table 805.

32. Dulce De Gevaudan, (b.c.1095-d.b.1130), **daughter of above,** married (1112), Raymond Berenger III, Count of Barcelona, (b.1080-d.1131). **Line 5 - Barcelona - Castile.**

Reference, RFC Line 257 and ES Vol. III., Table 805.

31. Berengaria of Barcelona, (b.c.1116-d.1149), **daughter of above,** married (1128), Alfonse VII, King of Castile, (b.1105-d.1157). **Line 1 - Burgundy - Castile.**

Reference, RFC Line 86 and ES Vol. II., Table 69.

30. Sancho III, King of Castile, (b.1134-d.1158), married (1151), Blanche of Navarre, (b.c.1134-d.1156), daughter of Garcia VI, King of Navarre, (b.c.1111-d.1150), **Line 3 - Asturias - Navarre,** who married (1)(c.1131), Marguerite of L'Aigle, (d.1141), daughter of Gilbert, Lord of L'Aigle, who married Julienne of Perche.

Reference, RFC Line 83 and ES Vol. II., Table 62.

29. Alfonso VIII, King of Castile, (b.1155-d.1214), married Eleanor of England, (b.1162-d.1214), daughter of Henry II, King of England. **Line 2 - Anjou - Plantagenet.**

Reference, RFC Line 83 and ES Vol. II., Table 62.

Blanche of Castile, (b.1188-d.1252), younger daughter.

Reference, ES Vol. II., Table 62.

Bibliography

Holy Blood, Holy Grail, by Michael Baigent, Richard Leigh, and Henry Lincoln. (1982).

The Messianic Legacy, by Michael Baigent, Richard Leigh, and Henry Lincoln. (1986).

Isenburg, Wilhelm Karl, Stammtafeln, Vol. I. (1953).

Royalty for Commoners, (RFC), by Roderick W. Stuart, Third Edition (1998).

Royalty for Commoners, (RFC), by Roderick W. Stuart, Fourth Edition (2002).

Europaische Stammtafeln, (ES), Vol. II., by Detlev Schwennicke, (1984).

Europaische Stammtafeln, (ES), Vol. III., Part 4, Tables 601-820, by Detlev Schwennicke, (1989).

Blanche of Castile and the Holy Blood Holy Grail

*

*   *

Printed in Great Britain
by Amazon

17732720R00047